jenny bristow
light
taste the good life

jenny bristow
light
taste the good life

THE
BLACKSTAFF
PRESS

BELFAST

IN ASSOCIATION WITH UTV

contents

soups

vegetarian

fish

meat

desserts

What we eat has a profound physical and emotional impact on us. Food is a source of pleasure and comfort and can contribute dramatically to our well-being. I've always believed that you are what you eat – if you eat well, you feel well. This philosophy is at the heart of my new book, *Jenny Bristow Light*. The recipes that I've gathered together here make the most of the goodness in all foods and use cooking methods that maximise the vitality and energy that good food can offer us.

Jenny Bristow Light is all about getting the best from our food. We know that high-fat cooking methods and too many rich foods are just not good for us. The recipes in this book are designed to help you choose and cook foods that will make you feel great. Fruit, vegetables, fish, cereals, pulses, grains and herbs are here in abundance, foods designed to ensure that you and your body get all the variety and nourishment you need. Dishes like sunshine cereal, mango and peach smoothie, roasted yellow pepper soup and middle-eastern saffron chicken look and taste fantastic – and they're good for you!

In my new collection you'll find new and easy ways to enhance the flavour and goodness of the food you eat and to keep the salt, fat and sugar content low. For example, the apple, lemon and vanilla cake is made with olive oil to reduce the saturated fat content; the lean lasagne has a tasty low-fat topping; and the balsamic syrup dressing is practically fat-free. Of course, being good to yourself also includes making sure that you indulge yourself now and again, so you'll find a fantastic range of desserts that will help you do just that! Try the gingered fruit crème brûlée or the cherry tart or, for a special occasion, the mouth watering marbled chocolate torte with white chocolate and marshmallow sauce – real mood food!

Although the recipes in this collection will suit practically everyone, I have been careful to include alternatives for those who suffer an intolerance to certain kinds of foods. There's advice and suggestions on how dishes can be adapted for those with gluten and lactose intolerance. I've also provided practical hints and tips on cooking methods that help you get the best out of food, and information on how particular kinds of food can contribute to health and well-being.

Jenny Bristow Light is for all those who love food and care about what they eat. I hope you enjoy the recipes – they're just the kind of thing that I make for myself at home and they're filled with the fun and joy that cooking and eating give me. So go on, treat yourself, and taste the good life!

Jenny Bristow

conversion tables

volume			weights			measurements	
1 tsp	5ml		grams	ounces		millimetres	inches
1 dsp	10ml		10g	^{1}/2oz		3mm	^{1}/8 inch
1 tbsp	15ml		25g	1oz		5mm	^{1}/4 inch
55ml	2floz		40g	1^1/2oz		1cm	^{1}/2 inch
75ml	3floz		50g	2oz		2cm	^{3}/4 inch
125ml	4floz		60g	2^1/2oz		2.5cm	1 inch
150ml	^{1}/4pt		75g	3oz		3cm	1^1/4 inches
275ml	^{1}/2pt		110g	4oz		4cm	1^1/2 inches
425ml	^{3}/4pt		125g	4^1/2oz		4.5cm	1^3/4 inches
570ml	1pt		150g	5oz		5cm	2 inches
1 litre	1^3/4pt		175g	6oz		7.5cm	3 inches
			200g	7oz		10cm	4 inches
			225g	8oz		13cm	5 inches
			250g	9oz		15cm	6 inches
			275g	10oz		18cm	7 inches
			350g	12oz		20cm	8 inches
			400g	14oz		23cm	9 inches
			450g	1lb		25cm	10 inches
			700g	1^1/2lb		28cm	11 inches
			900g	2lb		30cm	12 inches
			1.3kg	3lb			
			1.8kg	4lb			
			2.3kg	5lb			

oven temperatures

degrees centigrade	gas mark
140°	1
150°	2
170°	3
180°	4
190°	5
200°	6
220°	7
230°	8
240°	9

change to a healthier lifestyle

So many discussions of diet and healthy lifestyle focus exclusively on food as something physical, ignoring the other hungers that good food satisfies, such as our need for comfort and well-being, and the connections it establishes between ourselves and friends, family and the natural world. We love food for the sensual pleasure it gives, for its beauty, aromas, flavours and textures.

The Mediterranean diet is rooted in just such a view of food and over the years this philosophy has shown itself to be profoundly wise. People who live in these countries are among the healthiest in the world, have a low incidence of coronary disease and cancer and live longer. The Mediterranean diet is the model for my everyday diet, a diet based largely on plant foods such as vegetables, fruits, grains and pulses; on moderate amounts of fish, poultry, nuts and wine; on small amounts of red meat, saturated fat, dairy produce and sugar; and on a minimum of processed foods. This diet is inclusive, has plenty of choice and is well balanced.

Changing to a healthier lifestyle is not just about counting calories and carbohydrates or losing the fat content and therefore much of the taste of food. Rather, it's about limiting our consumption of the harmful saturated fats that increase cholesterol levels. These fats are found in dairy products and red meat, and in highly processed fast foods and convenience food snacks. Of course, foods of this type are still beneficial – red meat, for example, is rich in protein, iron and vitamins B6 and B12 – though it is worth using cooking methods or lower fat options that will keep the fat content to a minimum.

Living a healthier lifestyle then is really about a shift in balance towards foods such as olive oil, grains, vegetables, fruit and beans, which are low in saturated fat, high in fibre, and high in antioxidants that have been shown to help to prevent disease. In order to get the best out of them, buy fruit and vegetables that are in season and, even if it is a little more expensive, buy produce that is locally grown and organic – it is much better for you.

You should also ensure that your weekly diet contains a certain amount of Omega 3–rich fats, a particular type of polyunsaturated fat that can help prevent blood clotting. Omega 3 fatty acids are found in fish, particularly oily fish such as herring, salmon, mackerel and fresh tuna fish. It's also worth making sure that you eat yoghurt regularly as part of your diet. Low-fat and Greek-style yoghurts contain beneficial bacteria and enzymes that help the body digest food efficiently.

Of course, changing your diet is only part of living a healthier lifestyle. It goes without saying that regular physical activity is an essential part of staying well and healthy. So go on, what are you waiting for?

essential ingredients

oils

Olive oil varies in colour from golden yellow to deep green, depending on the olives used and the type of pressing, and is a must for your store cupboard. Because it is less processed and is rich in monosaturated fat it is much better for you than butter or any other cooking oils. Extra virgin olive oil comes from the first pressing of the olives. Its non-acidic fruity flavour makes it ideal for many dishes, and it is particularly good for dressings. This oil does not like very high temperatures – it will smoke easily and its flavour will be weakened. Use mainly for cooking at medium temperatures and for flavouring. If you are looking for a more neutral oil – extra virgin oil has quite a strong flavour – go for a vegetable oil such as sunflower or grapeseed. Peanut and nut oils have a very intense flavour and are often better for flavouring than cooking. Like sesame oil, they should be used very sparingly.

balsamic vinegar

There is no better way to add imagination and flavour to your cooking than with balsamic vinegar. This great favourite of mine from the Modena region of Italy is top of my list for an all-purpose vinegar. Choose the best you can afford – prices will vary considerably – as some of the cheaper ones have a rather rough flavour.

salt

Though you should be careful about the amount you consume, there is no doubt that salt is an excellent flavouring. Up until recently, table salt has been the salt most readily available and most commonly used here. Made from rock-salt deposits in sea beds, it often contains whitener and iodine. In recent times sea salt has become as popular as table salt. Pure and fresh, sea salt is made from evaporating sea water and needs to be used only sparingly. Fine or flaked sea salt is the easiest to use and this can be used to salt food even after the food is cooked. Do try to use as little salt as possible.

fresh herbs

No single ingredient has had a greater impact on our cooking over the last few years than fresh herbs and we now have a terrific selection in supermarkets, speciality shops and Asian markets. Simply wash, chop finely or coarsely and add to a dish according to taste. Each herb has its own special and beneficial properties and though you will find examples of these throughout the book it is well worth taking some time to explore them further. If at all possible, use herbs fresh the day you pick or buy them. Woody herbs such as rosemary, thyme and sage will keep for up to a week if wrapped in damp paper and stored in a plastic bag; softer-leafed herbs such as basil, tarragon and mint will keep for a shorter time. Don't forget the rather more exotic fresh ginger, lemon grass, galangal and Kaffir lime leaves. Remember, herbs are an excellent way of adding flavour without using salt.

dried spices and herbs

These add character, flavour and few calories to both sweet and savoury food. Ideal as a flavouring for stuffings, marinades, sauces and toppings. Dried spices and herbs should be replaced every six months as they tend to lose their strength.

pulses

Pulses is a collective term for peas, beans and lentils. Pulses are low in fat, high in protein and work as either main dishes or as accompaniments. They are excellent in stews, soups and salads. Try experimenting with different types of beans and lentils – for example, the less common puy lentils, tiny black lentils with an earthy flavour, are excellent in salads.

rice and grains

Rice and grains are low in fat, inexpensive and play an important part in a balanced diet. It's important to have a variety of these in your store cupboard. As far as rice goes, I always have a good supply of risotto rice, a creamy and comforting Italian rice; wild rice and long grain rice, great for salads and as an accompaniment to practically any dish; and aromatic Basmati rice, which is a must with curries and Indian dishes. Brown rice is also handy to have and is very high in fibre. Of the grains, I love couscous and bulgar wheat, grains that need very little cooking and can be eaten hot or cold – they're great in salads and stews. I also love polenta, with its wonderful yellow meal colour – it is excellent for sweet and savoury dishes and adds a great crunchiness to crumbles and pastries. Polenta is also gluten-free.

a few words on cooking utensils . . .

It's well worth investing in a good set of pans and some good-quality knives. Non-stick pots and/or those made of heavy-gauge metal are excellent for cooking. They disperse heat evenly, create an even colouring and develop the flavour of food without excessive amounts of fat. Non-stick grill pans and skillets are also very handy to have. A pre-heated grill pan sears food instantly and the raised ridged edges allow the fat to drain off easily. Good sharp knives are also a must – they will prevent bruising of fruit and vegetables, thus ensuring that they retain all their goodness. Buy knives that sharpen well and don't rust.

For me there are two kinds of breakfast – the weekday breakfast, **quick and easy**, and my weekend breakfast, **enjoyed at a leisurely pace**. A chance to make smoothies, muesli, breads, spiced fruit . . .

smoothies

Quick, easy and packed full of goodness, smoothies make an ideal breakfast. Whether you use fruit or vegetables, yoghurt or fruit juice, they will not only give you many of the vitamins you need, they'll also make you feel great.

To maximise your vitamin intake buy fruit and vegetables in season.

Smoothies are delicious poured over muesli instead of milk or yoghurt.

mango and peach

tangy and zesty – the perfect wake-up call

serves 1–2

2 ready-to-eat mangoes
2 peaches
juice of 1 large orange
250ml/^{1}/2pt plain yoghurt
juice of ^{1}/2 lemon (optional)
fresh mint and strawberry to garnish

Peel the mangoes and peaches and pare off the flesh from around the stone. Cut the flesh into small chunks and place in a blender. Add the orange juice and yoghurt and whiz. Add the lemon juice, if using, and stir. Pour the smoothie into some glasses. Serve decorated with fresh mint and a strawberry.

tropical treat

serves 2–3

1 small pineapple
2–3 oranges
1 banana
150ml/^{1}/4pt coconut milk
good handful of crushed ice

Cut the pineapple, oranges and banana into chunks. Add the fruit and the coconut milk to a blender or smoothie maker and whiz until you have a smooth mixture. Place the ice in some glasses and pour in the smoothie. If you wish, decorate with tropical fruit and mint leaves.

cranberry and apple sparkle

225g/8oz cranberries
275ml/½pt water
25g/1oz caster sugar
150ml/¼pt apple juice
pinch of cinnamon
110g/4oz fresh raspberries
110g/4oz blueberries

serves 2–3

An excellent source of vitamins A and C and known to help maintain a healthy urinary tract, cranberries are a very healthy addition to a balanced diet. Try making this refreshing drink at least once a week.

Pour the water and sugar into a saucepan. Add the cranberries and poach for 6–8 minutes until the cranberries have softened. Remove from the heat and leave to cool. Pour the mixture into a freezer tray and place in the freezer for 2 hours until chilled and slushy.

Place a quarter of the iced cranberries in a blender with the apple juice, cinnamon and half of the raspberries. Whiz until smooth.

Place the remaining iced cranberries in a glass along with the remaining raspberries and the blueberries. Pour the blended cinnamon drink over the fruit and serve at once.

serves 1

tropical fruit lassi

½ melon
2 kiwis
110g/4oz strawberries
125ml/¼pt chilled yoghurt or milk
½ pomegranate

Traditionally, a lassi is an Indian yoghurt drink designed to refresh in hot weather. I have adapted this idea to create a yoghurt drink that's packed with vitamin C and certain to give you the vitality boost you need. Soya or rice milk may also be used in this recipe.

Cut the melon into chunks and place in a blender. Add the kiwi fruit, strawberries and yoghurt or milk and whiz for 30 seconds. Crush and add the pomegranate seeds and give the lassi a good stir. Chill if desired.

vegetable juices

carrot surprise

This vitamin-rich breakfast drink is packed with healthy ingredients. The betacarotene content in the carrots is a good source of vitamin A and helps to boost the immune system, while the wheat-germ oil is packed with vitamin E, which is good for your skin.

3–4 carrots – peeled and chopped
1 stick celery
1 grapefruit – any variety
1–2 tsp wheat-germ oil
ice cubes to serve

Place everything in a blender, except the ice, and whiz until smooth. Place the ice in two glasses and pour in the carrot surprise. Serve immediately.

tasty tomato juice

High in vitamin C, tomatoes can be used to make a great drink.

4 medium ripe tomatoes
2 apples – peeled, cored and quartered
150ml/^{1}/4pt unsweetened apple juice
juice of 1 lime
^{1}/2 inch root ginger – peeled and grated
handful crushed ice

Place the tomatoes, apples, apple juice, lime juice and ginger in a blender and whiz gently. Place the crushed ice in two glasses and pour the tomato juice over. This juice may also be served warm – simply heat gently for 1 minute.

Cereals are a great source of protein, carbohydrates and vitamins and are perfect breakfast food. This sunshine cereal is made with oats, which are high in protein and calcium, and sunflower seeds, which are a good source of vitamin E. The dried apricots and raisins will give you a good natural energy boost to start your day.

Rye and barley contain gluten, so are not suitable for those who are gluten intolerant.

sunshine cereal
of toasted grain and nuts

serves 2–3

Mix together the rye flakes, oats, sunflower seeds and almonds in a bowl. Heat the oil in a pan and add the honey and cinnamon and stir well. Add the grains and continue cooking over a gentle heat until they are well coated.

Transfer the mixture to a baking sheet and spread out evenly. Bake in the oven @ 170°C/ gas mark 3 for 15 minutes until lightly browned, tossing occasionally during roasting.

Remove from the oven, allow to cool, then place in a large bowl. Add the dried fruit and mix w ell. The cereal can be stored in an airtight container for up to two weeks.

50g/2oz rye flakes
110g/4oz rolled porridge oats
25g/1oz sunflower seeds
25g/1oz sliced almonds
50g/1oz sunflower oil
4 dsp honey or maple syrup
pinch cinnamon
50g/2oz raisins
50g/2oz dried apricots or apples

honeyed yoghurt
with balsamic roasted peaches

serves 1–2

2–3 peaches – stoned and sliced
1 tbsp light brown sugar
2 tbsp balsamic vinegar
275ml/1/2pt yoghurt
2tbsp honey

This breakfast dish is a real treat. I've used roasted peaches for this recipe, but fresh berries also work very well. Choose yoghurt to suit your taste – a low-fat variety or a luxurious creamy-textured Greek yoghurt or an organic yoghurt.

Place the balsamic vinegar, brown sugar and peaches in a shallow pan. Cook for 2 minutes on the hob, or 10–12 minutes in the oven @ 200°C/gas mark 6, stirring occasionally. Remove from the heat and set to one side until ready to serve. Serve warm or cold.

Place the yoghurt in bowls or glasses and top with the softened peaches. Drizzle with honey.

This spiced fruit salad is very versatile. It's delicious served on its own but for a more filling breakfast try adding yoghurt and/or muesli.

spiced roasted fruit
with honey and orange syrup

4–6 peaches
4 nectarines
6–8 plums
6 figs – fresh or dried
6 apricots – fresh or dried
4 pears – fresh or dried
110g/4oz mixed dried fruit

spiced roasted fruit

Wash the fruit and remove all stones. Leave the small fruit whole and half or quarter any of the bigger fruit. Place in an ovenproof dish.

zest and juice of 2 oranges
2 tbsp honey
1 cinnamon stick – broken in half
3–4 star anise
2 cardamom pods

honey and orange syrup

Place the orange juice and zest in a small bowl and mix with the honey, cinnamon stick and star anise. Shell the cardamom pods, crush the seeds, add to the bowl and mix well. Pour the syrup over the fruits and roast in the oven @ 200ºC/gas mark 6 for 20–25 minutes, spooning the syrup over the fruit regularly during cooking. When the fruit has softened and blackened slightly, remove from the oven. Serve hot or cold.

The Glycaemic Index is a system for classifying carbohydrates according to the rate at which your body breaks them down and converts them into energy. Food that is classed as having a low GI factor is said to help the body burn fat more easily. Apples, grapes, kiwi fruit, oranges, peaches, pears and plums have a low GI factor while apricots, bananas, mangoes, paw-paw, pineapple, sultanas and raisins have a medium to high GI factor.

Walnut bread, with its wonderful colour and interesting flavour, is often made with yeast.
This version is simpler and yeast-free – the texture is less chewy but the flavour is still great. Increase the amount of walnuts if you prefer a more nutty flavour.

walnut
bread

serves 8–10

This bread can be made using a 450g/1lb loaf tin or a round tin, 15–18cm/6–7 inches in diameter. Grease and line the tin well.

Beat together the eggs and sugar until light and fluffy. The volume will be less with this dark brown sugar than it would be with caster sugar.

Sieve together the flour, baking powder and baking soda. Add to the egg mixture in 3 or 4 stages, alternating each stage with an addition of milk. Mix well between additions. When the flour and milk have been added, add the walnuts and mix well.

Transfer the bread to the lined greased tin and bake in the oven @ 180°C/gas mark 4 for approximately 45 minutes. When cooked, the loaf should become golden, firm to the touch and leave the side of the tin. Turn out and wrap in a clean dry tea towel to cool.

note

The choice of milk will affect the volume of the loaf. Full-cream milk will allow the loaf to rise higher and will give it more volume.

2 large eggs
50g/2oz dark brown Barbados sugar
450g/1lb strong plain flour
1 1/2tsp baking powder
1 1/2tsp baking soda
275ml/1/2pt milk – full-cream or semi-skimmed
110g/4oz walnuts – some finely, some coarsley chopped

I love this bread, with its swirling pattern and spicy sweetness. Vary the quantity of cinnamon depending on how much you like it.

rolled cinnamon
scone bread

serves 6–7

Grease well a round 18–20cm/7–8 inch tin and dust lightly with caster sugar.

Sieve the flour into a large bowl and add the baking powder if necessary. Cut and rub in the polyunsaturated fat until the mixture resembles fine breadcrumbs. Add the sugar, egg and milk and mix to a firm dough. Turn out onto a floured surface, knead lightly and roll out to a rectangular shape, approximately 30 x 23cm/12 x 9 inches and 1/2 inch thick.

450g/1lb plain flour + 2 tsp baking powder
or
450g/1lb cake-making self-raising flour
25g/1oz polyunsaturated fat
12 1/2g/1/2oz caster sugar
2 eggs – lightly beaten
125ml/1/4pt milk – full-cream or low-fat

filling

Make the filling by creaming together the fat, sugar and cinnamon powder. When it is smooth, spread it over the dough evenly.

50g/2oz softened butter or polyunsaturated fat
50g/2oz muscovado sugar
3 tsp good quality cinnamon powder

Brush around the edges of the dough with cold water – this will help seal the edges – and roll the dough up loosely into a log shape, making sure it is even and well-shaped. Using a sharp knife, cut the log into 7 slices and arrange flat in the tin with one in the centre.

Bake in the oven @ 200°C/gas mark 6 for 15–20 minutes until risen and golden. Remove from the tin and leave to cool. The scones will retain their individual roly-poly shape and can be separated easily

topping

This bread can also be given a topping for added flavour. Beat together the cream cheese, sugar, lemon juice and milk until smooth. When the cake is almost cooled, spread the topping over the cinnamon swirls and serve.

110g/4oz light cream cheese
50g/2oz icing sugar
2–3 tsp milk
2 tsp lemon juice

21

This is my healthy version of French toast, made with ciabatta or any of the other healthy breads now available, low-fat milk, and lots of fruit. You will need unsliced bread to make this French toast. Serve with yoghurt or fromage frais.

french
toast
stuffed with plums and peaches

Place the fruit in a large bowl with the maple syrup. If the fruit is very firm it should be poached gently for 1–2 minutes just to soften it slightly and then mixed with the maple syrup.

In a separate bowl whisk together the eggs, milk and vanilla extract.

Cut 4 slices of bread, each about $1/2$ inch thick. Cut each slice along one side to form a pocket. Use around half of the filling to fill the pockets, then seal the openings by pressing the bread firmly together. Place the fruit sandwiches on a flat dish and pour over the egg mixture, ensuring that each of the sandwiches is coated on both sides.

Heat the fat in a frying pan and add the sandwiches. Cook until both sides are golden.

Remove from the pan and place on some kitchen paper to absorb any excess oil. Cut the sandwich in half and serve with a spoonful of yoghurt on the side.

This recipe can also be used for savoury snacks. Simply fill the bread with ham, asparagus and sliced mushrooms.

2 peaches – stoned and sliced
2 plums or apricots – stoned and sliced
1 dsp maple syrup
2 eggs – lightly beaten
2 dsp low-fat milk
few drops of vanilla extract
4 slices bread
25g/1oz polyunsaturated fat

Plums, peaches and apricots, like most fruit, are high in vitamin C. Plums and apricots are particularly beneficial because they are also high in fibre. Plums are useful for improving circulation and can help to combat fluid retention.

oatmeal breakfast muffins

makes 10

These breakfast muffins are low in sugar and high in fibre to give you the perfect start to your day. To make them even healthier, you could replace the sugar with artificial sweetener or add a little banana or dried fruit for extra natural sweetness.

110g/4oz muscatel raisins
juice of 1 orange or 4 dsp
    unsweetened apple juice
75g/3oz rolled/porridge oats
175g/6oz self-raising flour
25g/1oz muscovado sugar or 1 tsp
    artificial sweetener, e.g. saccharin
$^1/_2$ tsp nutmeg
$^1/_2$ tsp cinnamon
2 tbsp grapeseed or sunflower oil
1 egg – lightly beaten
175ml/6floz buttermilk
cinnamon and icing sugar for dusting

Place the raisins in a small bowl with some of the juice for 10–15 minutes until they have plumped up.

Place the oats, flour, sugar or sweetener, nutmeg and cinnamon in a separate bowl and mix well. Add the raisins and any remaining juice and the oil, egg and buttermilk. Mix lightly for 1 minute only, then transfer to lined muffin tins and bake in the oven @ 200°C/gas mark 6 for 20–25 minutes. When cooked, remove from the tins and wrap in a clean, dry towel until they cool. Mix the cinnamon and icing sugar and use to dust the muffins.

A combination of fresh and dried fruit ensures a healthy amount of vitamins and minerals, especially vitamin C, betacarotene, potassium and iron. Fruit is also rich in fibre.

toasted muffins
with caramelised banana and coconut

1 muffin – cut in half and toasted
1–2 bananas – sliced
juice of 1/2 lemon
1 tsp honey
25g/1oz demerara sugar
1 dsp dessicated coconut
natural yoghurt

Arrange the bananas on top of the muffin halves. Drizzle with lemon juice and honey and sprinkle with sugar. Dust with the coconut and brown under a hot grill until the top starts to caramelise. Serve with a spoonful of yoghurt.

Bananas are great for breakfasts and for healthy snacks because they provide a good energy boost and are virtually fat free. Because they are easy to peel, they make a particularly good snack for kids.

tropical toasted bagels

2 bagels
1 mango
1 banana or peach
1 dsp mango relish
juice of 1/2 orange
1/2 inch root ginger – peeled and grated

Cut the bagels in half and toast under a hot grill.
Peel and dice the mango and banana and place in a large bowl.
Add the relish, orange juice and ginger. Spoon the fruit over the toasted bagel and toast under a hot grill until golden.

A healthy breakfast snack that provides an alternative to sugar-filled jams and jellies. I've used mangoes and bananas here, but choose fruit that is seasonal, fresh and ripe to give the best of flavour.

This is the perfect weekend breakfast. The fritters are tasty and easy to make and the batter can be prepared a couple of days in advance – just store it in the fridge. To give these fritters extra texture I've added a little red onion along with the bacon.

bacon
fritters
with roasted tomatoes and soft scrambled eggs

bacon fritters

Sieve the flour, baking powder and cayenne pepper into a bowl. Add the eggs and milk and mix well until the mixture forms a smooth yet quite stiff batter. When you are ready to make the fritters, add the onion and bacon and mix well.

Place the olive oil in a hot frying pan and then add 2 tbsp batter to form a small fritter. You should be able to fit 3–4 fritters in the pan. Cook for 2 minutes until golden, then turn and cook for the same amount of time on the other side. Remove and place on some kitchen paper to absorb any excess oil. Set to one side and keep warm. Continue with this process until all the batter mixture has been used.

110g/4oz plain flour
1 tsp baking powder
1/2 tsp cayenne pepper
2 eggs – lightly beaten
6 dsp semi-skimmed milk
1/2 red onion – finely diced
6 rashers grilled bacon – finely chopped
1 dsp olive oil

roasted tomatoes

Place the tomatoes on a grill tray and sprinkle with olive oil. Season and place under a hot grill for 2–3 minutes until roasted and slightly blackened.

2 tomatoes – halved
1 tbsp extra virgin olive oil
pinch sea salt
pinch freshly ground black pepper

scrambled eggs

Place the eggs, milk and paprika in a bowl and mix well. Melt the butter in a small non-stick pan and add the egg mixture. Cook for approximately 1 minute, stirring occasionally, until set but not overcooked. Serve immediately with the bacon fritters, roasted tomatoes and, if you wish, some grilled vegetables.

2–3 eggs
4 dsp semi-skimmed milk
1/4 tsp paprika
12 1/2g/1/2oz butter

snacks & salads

Light, satisfying and **good for you** at any time of day, these **snacks and salads** are ideal for increasing your intake of **fruit, vegetables, pulses** and **oily fish**.

If you prepare them yourself, pizzas can be one of the best fast foods around. This recipe is quick and easy and makes two pizza bases, so that one can be frozen and used at your convenience. I've included a few suggestions for toppings but really you can use whatever you fancy.

• thin and crispy
pizza

makes 2 large pizza bases

225g/8oz soda bread or self-raising flour
a good pinch of freshly ground black pepper
1dsp olive oil
150ml/^{1}/4pt low-fat milk and water mixed

Sieve the flour and pepper into a large bowl and add the olive oil and milky liquid. Mix until the ingredients start to come together as a soft dough. Turn the dough out onto a floured surface and knead gently to remove any cracks. Divide the dough and shape into two thin, flat rounds. Brush the top of each with just a hint of olive oil and bake in a hot oven @ 200°C/gas mark 6 for 15–20 minutes. Remove from the oven and wrap in a tea towel until cool.

tomato and basil

Arrange a handful of torn basil leaves, 6–8 slices ripe sliced tomatoes and 1 tbsp finely chopped red onion on top of the pizza. Eat on its own or grill for 1–2 minutes.

mexican style

In a bowl, mix 2 dsp chopped tomatoes, 1 dsp tomato puree, 1 tsp chilli sauce, ^{1}/2 finely chopped red onion and 1 dsp of sweet corn. Spread the mixture over the pizza base, top with 25g/1oz grated reduced-fat cheese, and pop under the grill for 1–2 minutes.

pesto with sardines or salami

Pre-heat the grill and spread the pizza base with 1 tsp pesto (see recipe on page 58) and add 2–3 sardines or a few slices of low-fat salami. Top with some feta or mozzarella cheese and grill for 3–4 minutes. Garnish with some parsley and/or a twist of lemon.

scorched flat bread
with roasted tomatoes,
olives and herb salad

bread of choice
110g/4oz black olives
1/2 red onion – finely chopped
1 clove garlic – finely chopped
10–12 cherry tomatoes
1 dsp olive oil
flat-leaf parsley or coriander to garnish

Place some bread on a hot grill pan for 1–2 minutes.

Mix together all the ingredients for the salad with olive oil, pile high on top of the scorched bread and place below a hot grill to cook for 2 minutes. Garnish with flat-leaf parsley or coriander.

Fluffy naans, focaccias, pittas and tortillas are all perfect for scorching on a hot grill pan and topping or filling with a really tasty salad. If you want something more filling, a few sardines or some slices of salami can be served on top of this open sandwich.

See also page 40 for a flat bread recipe.

Cooking tomatoes really boosts their nutritional value – in fact, cooked tomatoes are every bit as good for you as raw tomatoes. The cooking process increases the amount of lycopene, a powerful antioxidant that helps combat cancer and reduces the risk of heart disease by lowering cholesterol.

This rustic cheese sandwich goes perfectly with a tomato and pear relish. For a more filling snack, try teaming this sandwich with soup.

cheesy bruschetta
with a chunky pear relish

pear relish

Place all the ingredients in a large saucepan and bring to the boil. Cover and simmer gently for 45 minutes. This long slow cooking is important to concentrate the flavour of the relish and will ensure that the vinegar loses its sharp flavour. By the end of the cooking time, the relish will have thickened. Remove the cinnamon stick and allow the relish to cool. When cooled, place the relish in a sterile jar and use when required. Serve hot or cold. The relish will keep for 2 weeks if stored in an airtight container.

3 pears – peeled and chopped
375g/13oz tin chopped tomatoes
110g/4oz soft brown sugar
150ml/¼pt raspberry vinegar
1 tsp chilli sauce
1 tsp salt
1 cinnamon stick – broken in half
1 small onion – finely chopped
1 inch root ginger – peeled and grated

cheesy bruschetta

Spread the bread lightly with the mustard. Top two of the slices with mozzarella and cover with the remaining two slices. Dip the sandwiches in the beaten egg and make sure they are well coated. Shake off any excess egg mixture.

Heat the oil in a frying pan and add the sandwiches. Cook for 2–3 minutes, turning once, until the sandwiches are crisp and golden on the outside. Remove from the pan and place on a little kitchen paper to remove any excess oil.

Place the sandwiches on a plate and cut in half to reveal the soft melting cheese. Serve at once with the pear relish and some mixed leaves.

4 thin slices of crusty bread or ciabatta
½ tsp mustard
110g/4oz buffalo mozzarella – thinly sliced
1 egg – beaten
1 dsp olive oil

chargrilled pear and bacon sandwich
with a warm honeyed chilli dressing

serves 1–2

Sandwiches are great snacking food and this warm toasted sandwich is particularly delicious. Feel free to change the bread to suit yourself and to substitute the pear with whatever fruit is in season. Nectarines and peaches also work very well with bacon.

1 red chilli – deseeded and very finely chopped
2 dsp honey
1 tsp wholegrain mustard

2 pears – skin on, cored, cut into thick slices
2 red apples – skin on, cored, cut into thick slices
2 slices wholemeal bread – thickly sliced
2–4 slices cooked bacon or Parma ham
lamb's lettuce to garnish

Mix together the chilli, honey and mustard in a bowl. Place the dressing in a small saucepan and heat gently for 1 minute.

Drizzle the pear and apple slices with a little of the dressing, then place on grill pan for a couple of minutes until the fruit is softened and a little charred.

Assemble the sandwich by toasting the bread, sprinkling it with a little of the dressing and topping it with the apples and pears. Now add the bacon or Parma ham and garnish with lamb's lettuce. Pour over the remainder of the warm dressing and serve at once.

balsamic syrup dressing

When it is heated, balsamic vinegar caramelises and takes on a wonderful sweet and sour flavour. It is not necessary to use expensive balsamic vinegar for this recipe.

275ml/½pt balsamic vinegar
1 dsp spring onions
pinch of paprika

Pour the balsamic vinegar into a small saucepan, cover, and bring to the boil. Continue boiling until the vinegar has reduced by half and become syrupy. Allow to cool, then add the spring onions and paprika. Ideal over green salad and as a sauce over chargrilled steak or chicken. This dressing will keep for 1–2 weeks if stored in an airtight container.

orange minted salad

6–8 oranges – peeled and thickly sliced
1 blood orange – peeled and thinly sliced
2 dsp orange blossom honey
1 red or white onion – finely sliced
1/2 tsp cinnamon powder
good handful of mint – roughly chopped

serves 6

Place the oranges in a serving bowl. To make the dressing, reserve any juice that has come out of the oranges during slicing and place it in a saucepan. Add the honey and heat gently for 2–3 minutes. Sprinkle the oranges with the sliced onions, dust with cinnamon powder and pour the dressing over. Mix well and place in the fridge for 15 minutes to chill. Garnish with mint just before serving.

A clean and refreshing salad that is ideal with curries or any spiced dish.

herb-crusted toast with goat's cheese
pan-cooked leeks and tarragon

2 tsp olive oil or butter
2 tsp tarragon – roughly chopped
2 leeks – finely sliced
1/2 tsp chilli flakes
freshly ground black pepper

4 slices crusty bread – thinly sliced
110g/4oz goat's cheese
1 tsp mustard
fresh tarragon to garnish

serves 2

Heat half of the olive oil or butter in a shallow frying pan and add the leeks, chilli flakes, half of the tarragon and a good grinding of black pepper. Cook over a low heat for approximately 10–12 minutes until the leeks have softened and absorbed the flavour of the herbs.

Sprinkle the bread on one side with the rest of the olive oil and tarragon and brown below a hot grill. Place two slices of the toasted bread on a plate and pile the leeks on top. Crumble the goat's cheese over the leeks and place the sandwich under a hot grill until the cheese is bubbling and golden. Spread the other two slices of bread with mustard and place them on top of the goat's cheese and leeks to create two sandwiches. Cut in half and serve garnished with tarragon and some lettuce on the side.

This sandwich is delicious with the chunky pear relish on page 33.

It's hard to think of anything better than the flavour of slow-cooked leeks and creamy goat's cheese.

beetroot salad

Beetroot is one of my favourite vegetables — it's healthy, has a sweet nutty flavour and is a glorious colour. Fresh beetroot is now widely available in vegetable shops and in supermarkets. I love roasting beetroot as it intensifies its nutty flavour but you can also boil or steam it. Boiling is the quicker method and provided the skins are not ruptured, the colour of the cooked beetroot will be excellent. Ensure that beetroot are ripe when you buy them — they should be slightly soft — or they can take forever to cook!

8–10 small beetroots
8–10 shallots – peeled
2 dsp olive oil
4 dsp balsamic vinegar
2 tsp chilli sauce
1 dsp honey
freshly ground black pepper
110–175g/4–6oz goat's cheese
lamb's lettuce or chives

Wash the beetroots carefully. Do not rupture the skin. Place them in a roasting tin with the shallots and drizzle with the olive oil, vinegar, honey and chilli sauce. Now give the vegetables a good sprinkling of black pepper and mix everything well. Cover the dish with some tinfoil and bake in the oven @ 200°C/gas mark 6 for approximately 1–1½ hours. Cooking times will vary — when cooked the beetroot should be tender and the skin should peel off easily. Give the vegetables a stir now and again during cooking and spoon the juices over the beetroot.

When the vegetables are cooked and tender remove the roasting tin from the oven. Allow the vegetables to cool a little, then slice the shallots. Gently remove the skin from the beetroots, cut them into chunks and place them in a bowl with the sliced onions.

Strain the roasting juices from the tin. If necessary, add a little extra virgin olive oil and honey to taste. Spoon the juice over the vegetables.

To assemble the dish, place the beetroots on a plate. Top with goat's cheese and pop under the grill for 1–2 minutes. Then arrange the shallots around the outside. The goat's cheese can also be grilled separately, cut into chunks and scattered over the salad. Finish the dish off with a good grinding of black pepper and sprinkle with lamb's lettuce or chives.

Beetroot is a wonderful vegetable — low in fat, high in fibre and full of great health benefits. Full of vitamins A, B and C along with calcium, iron and potassium, beetroot is good in a balanced diet if you are trying to lower high blood pressure or to protect against anaemia.

Clockwise from top:
orange minted salad;
cucumber, coriander,
tomato and red onion
salad; and beetroot salad

A wonderfully fresh and lively salad tossed in a delicious basil pesto dressing. This salad looks attractive served on a large platter.

mediterranean
salad

If you find the flavour of fresh raw onion too strong, then slice the onions and place in a bowl of slightly salted cold water for 30 minutes before using. Drain them, pat dry and dust them with 1 tsp soft brown sugar – works a treat.

Place the tomatoes and peppers under a hot grill for approximately 2 minutes, turning occasionally, until they are blackened and sweetened. Deseed and slice the peppers and set them and the tomatoes to one side.

Spread the rocket leaves and basil on a large serving platter and scatter the tomatoes and peppers on top.

Lightly boil the peas for 2–3 minutes and sprinkle over the platter.

Crumble the feta and scatter the olives and onion over the salad.

Finally, toast the pine nuts for a few minutes in a pan until they are lightly browned and sprinkle over the dish.

4–5 tomatoes
1–2 yellow peppers
rocket leaves
good handful basil
110g/4oz fresh garden peas
225g/8oz feta cheese
110g/4oz large green olives
1/2 red onion – finely sliced
110g/4oz toasted pine nuts

pesto dressing

Place all the ingredients, except the salt and pepper, in a food processor and blend until you have a smooth mixture. Taste and season. Drizzle the dressing over the salad and serve immediately.

25g/1oz basil
25g/1oz pine nuts
25g/1oz Parmesan
2 tsp garlic – chopped
150ml/1/4pt olive oil
juice of 1 lemon
salt and freshly ground
   black pepper

I love the texture and flavour of this salad and its crunchy rustic appearance.

cucumber, coriander, tomato and red onion salad

Make the dressing by mixing together the oil, vinegar, honey and black pepper. Set to one side.

To make the croutons, chop the bread into even sized chunks and toast lightly under a hot grill until golden and crispy.

Mix all the salad ingredients together with the croutons.

Add the coriander to the dressing and pour it over the salad. Toss lightly and garnish with coriander.

1 tsp extra virgin olive oil
2 tsp balsamic vinegar
1 dsp honey
freshly ground black pepper
1 small loaf of crusty bread
2 large tomatoes – deseeded and diced
25g/1oz green or black olives
1 small red onion – coarsely sliced
1/2 cucumber – peeled and diced
1 dsp fresh coriander – coarsely chopped
fresh coriander to garnish

Quick and easy to cook, this is ideal barbeque food.

warm sundried tomato and potato salad

Place the potatoes in a steamer and cook for 8–10 minutes until they are almost tender. Now, place them in a large bowl and mix with the sundried tomatoes, oil, paprika and herbs. Divide the mixture into 6 servings and wrap each portion in a secure foil parcel. Place on the barbeque and cook for 8–10 minutes until hot, bubbling and cooked. Serve.

450g/1lb red or baby potatoes – skin on, cut into chunks
8–10 sundried tomatoes – sliced
2 dsp oil – use the oil that the sundried tomatoes are served in
1 tsp paprika
basil or parsley

A quick and easy snack that brings together lots of wonderful flavours. The creamy mustard dressing finishes the dish off a treat. This dough will make two large flat breads. If making the gluten-free flat bread you may find it easier to work with and shape 4–5 smaller breads.

flat bread with chargrilled chicken

avocado and roasted peppers

serves 2

flat bread

Mix together the flour and add the oil and liquid. Mix to form a soft dough. Divide the dough into 2 pieces and shape into rounds. Flatten out into flat breads approximately 18cm/7 inches in diameter. Cook each one individually in a frying pan or grill pan. If you are using a frying pan, it will need to be lightly oiled. Cook for 1–2 minutes on each side until lightly cooked and golden. If sealed in a polythene bag, the flat bread will keep for 4–5 days.

175g/6oz plain flour
1 tbsp olive oil
75–100ml/3–3^1/2floz water or milk

gluten-free variation

Replace the plain flour with
50g/2oz gluten-free flour
110g/4oz soya or chick pea flour
1 tsp xanthan gum

topping

Cook the chicken fillet on a hot grill pan for 8–9 minutes until nicely charred and cooked. Cut into fairly large bite-sized pieces. While the chicken is cooking, fry the pepper for 4–5 minutes in a lightly oiled pan. Place the chicken and peppers in a bowl with the avocado, tomato, cucumber and olive oil and mix well.

1 chicken fillet
1 red pepper – cut into chunks
1 avocado – diced
1 beef tomato – sliced
^{1}/4 cucumber – sliced
1 tsp olive oil

creamy mustard dressing

Mix together the yoghurt, mustard, chilli flakes and pesto.

To assemble the dish, pile the chicken and avocado topping onto the tortilla and smother with the creamy mustard dressing. Serve hot or cold.

4 dsp yoghurt
^{1}/2 tsp mustard
^{1}/2 tsp chilli flakes
1 tsp red pesto

spicy beanfeast

serves 2

Peas, beans and lentils are not only delicious, they're also fantastically good for you. Full of protein and fibre, this spicy beanfeast is a filling and healthy snack that is guaranteed to satisfy. I've used tinned beans in this recipe for speed and convenience but if possible, use dried beans or peas. The flavour is much better. Just ensure that the beans are fully cooked by the time you are ready to begin this recipe. Be careful to follow the instructions on packets of beans carefully. Most beans require soaking overnight.

1 tsp olive oil
1 onion – thickly sliced
2 tomatoes – cut into chunks
1 tsp turmeric
2 tsp curry powder
1 tin haricot or cannellini beans or chickpeas or a combination of all three
2 dsp water or stock
2 slices garlic or naan bread

natural yoghurt
wedges of tomato

Heat the oil in a saucepan and add the onion, tomatoes, turmeric and curry powder and cook for 3–4 minutes. Add the beans and/or chickpeas and heat through for a further 1–2 minutes. Add the liquid to the mixture and cook until everything is piping hot.

When everything is nearly ready, warm the bread gently under the grill or in a pre-heated oven. Place the bread on a plate and pile the beanfeast on top. Garnish with natural yoghurt and wedges of tomato.

sundried tomato and pine nut scones

and blueberry and chocolate scones

makes 6

225g/8oz plain flour
1 tsp baking powder
25g/1oz margarine

gluten-free variation

110g/4oz gluten-free flour and
110g/4oz soya/brown rice/potato flour
1 tsp gluten-free baking powder
1 tsp xanthan gum
25g/1oz margarine

Mix the flour in a bowl and add the baking powder and, if required, xanthan gum. Mix well. Cut and rub in the margarine until the mixture resembles a crumble.

tomato and pine nut

If making sundried tomato and pine nut scones add 50g/2oz chopped sundried tomatoes, 25g/1oz toasted pine nuts, 1 egg and 150ml/^{1}/4pt buttermilk. Mix to a firm but soft dough.

blueberry and chocolate

If making blueberry and chocolate scones, add 25g/1oz sugar, 50g/1oz dried blueberries, 25g/1oz white chocolate and 150ml/^{1}/4pt buttermilk. Mix to a firm but soft dough. If you wish, a little egg may be added to enrich the dough.

Turn the scone mixture out onto a floured table, cut into even-sized pieces and shape into rounds. Place on a baking sheet and bake in the oven @ 200°C/gas mark 6 for 15–20 minutes. Wrap in a tea towel and serve warm or cold.

Xanthan or xanthan gum is a product which is gluten-free and is very good for baking, making the texture of bread and scones less crumbly. It should be added with the dry ingredients before adding any liquids. Brown rice flour is very good for savoury scones and soya flour for sweet ones. Gluten-free baking powder is readily available.

43

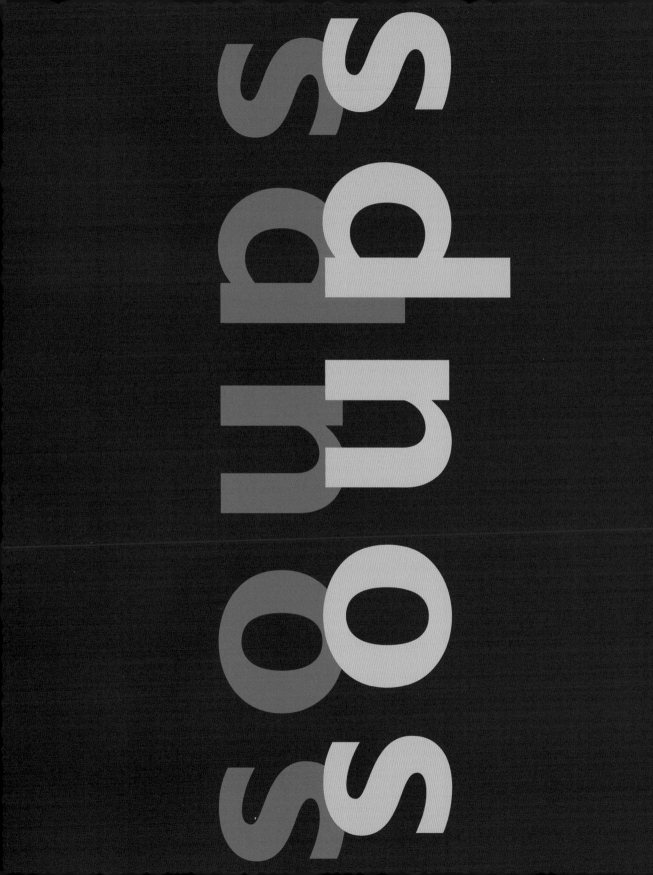

Soups to **inspire** you, whether you want a starter for a dinner party or you're just in need of a **moreish comfort** food. Packed with **goodness**, bursting with **flavour** and made with simple, **wholesome** ingredients, what more **honest good** food is there?

stocks

Homemade stock is never quite the trouble it sounds and is well worth the effort. It is the basis for any good soup and gives a subtle, light flavour to risottos, stews and sauces. It can be made in advance and in fairly large quantities and stored in the freezer for use at a later stage. If possible, try to avoid using stock cubes – they are very strong in flavour and high in salt. Many health and whole food shops now sell healthier options but do check the labels for salt content. These alternatives are better for you than traditional stock cubes, but they are still a poor second to homemade varieties in terms of flavour and nutrition

tips for making low-fat stock

- Remove any skin or fat from bones or chicken joints before using them to make stock.
- Using bones, giblets or carcass will generate more fat than if you are making a vegetable stock. As with all stocks, the fat will rise to the surface and can be skimmed off with a spoon during cooking. Skimming is easier if you allow the stock to cool after cooking as the fat will settle on the surface. If possible, leave the stock to cool overnight in the fridge. By the next day the fat will have solidified and can be easily removed.
- Be sure to simmer your stock. Do not overcook or boil rapidly as this can make the stock cloudy and will spoil the appearance of light soups.
- To increase the flavour of vegetable stock, add fennel or tomatoes in summer and mushrooms and red pepper in the winter.
- To intensify the flavour of homemade stock, simmer it gently over a long period until it has reduced down to one-third of the original volume. The handiest way to store stock concentrate of this type is in ice-cube trays – a cube or two will give dishes a fantastic injection of flavour.
- If freezing stock, allow it to cool and chill before freezing. Frozen stock will keep for up to three months.

quick vegetable stock

A quick vegetable stock can be made in 15 minutes. Place 2–3 stalks celery, an onion cut in half, a carrot, a few peppercorns, a bay leaf, a bunch of herbs and 570ml–1.2 litres/1–2pt water in a large saucepan. Cover and simmer gently for 15 minutes, skim, and strain off the liquid. Taste and season – the herbs may provide enough seasoning, especially if you add parsley stalks.

A recipe for chicken stock can be found on page 94.

roasted yellow
pepper soup
with basil cream

serves 6–8

6 yellow peppers – halved and deseeded
4 cloves garlic
handful of basil leaves

2 onions – finely chopped
2 shallots – finely chopped
4 cloves garlic – finely chopped
200g/7oz cherry tomatoes
125ml/4floz tomato juice
1.2 litres/2pt homemade vegetable stock

6–8 shredded basil leaves
1–2 tsp low fat fromage frais

This dramatic Mediterranean soup is ideal for dinner parties – the intense yellow colour of the peppers and the green of the basil cream look wonderful together. Full of flavour and packed with goodness, this soup is also ideal for those who are diabetic or watching the fat content of their food.

Place the peppers, basil and the whole cloves of garlic in a foil parcel and roast in the oven @ 200°C/gas mark 6 for 45 minutes until the flesh of the peppers has completely broken down and softened. Take out of the oven, discard the garlic and skin the peppers. Place the peppers and basil in a bowl. Drain the cooking juices and reserve in a separate bowl.

In a large saucepan dry fry the onions, shallots, garlic and roasted peppers. Cook for 5–6 minutes until the onion becomes softened. Add the cherry tomatoes, tomato juice, stock and cooking juices from the peppers and simmer gently for 12–15 minutes. Whiz the soup in a blender and return it to the saucepan. Re-heat and serve with a swirl of fromage frais mixed with some shredded basil.

Peppers are terrifically high in vitamin C. They are known to help boost the immune system and to help maintain a healthy heart and urinary tract.

oriental
spiced soup
with sweet red onion

serves 6

1 tsp olive oil
1 stalk of lemon grass – bruised
1 inch root ginger
1 medium potato – peeled and diced
1 small red onion – finely chopped
4 spring onions – finely chopped
1–2 tsp mildly spiced curry paste
2 x 400g/14oz tins coconut milk
570ml/1pt chicken stock

1 red onion
1 tsp olive oil
1 tsp soft brown sugar
handful of coriander to garnish

This mildly spiced soup has a sweet, creamy texture. The taste is quite delicate, so if you can, use fresh stock – it is so much lighter and less heavily seasoned than stock cubes.

Coconut milk has quite a high fat content, but light versions are now available and should be used where possible.

Heat the oil in large saucepan and add the lemon grass, ginger, potato, the red onion and the spring onions. Cover and cook gently for 4–5 minutes until slightly softened. Add the curry paste and continue cooking for 2–3 minutes. Next add the coconut milk and the stock. Stir well, reduce the heat and allow to simmer gently for 15–20 minutes until the potato is softened.

Remove the lemon grass and place the soup in a blender. Whiz until smooth. Return the soup to the saucepan and place on the hob to heat through.

sweet red onion

While the soup is heating, place the oil in a shallow pan and add the other red onion and the brown sugar. Cook gently for 2–3 minutes until the onion has softened and slightly blackened.

To serve, pour the soup into bowls and garnish with the sweet red onion and coriander.

fresh
mushroom
soup

25g/1oz butter or olive oil
2 cloves garlic – finely chopped
1 large onion – finely chopped
570g/1lb mushrooms – thickly chopped
1 tbsp sundried tomato paste
150ml/^{1}/4pt dry white wine
570ml/1pt light chicken stock
salt and freshly ground black pepper
4 dsp parsley – finely chopped

Heat the butter or oil in a heavy-based saucepan and add the garlic, onion and mushrooms. Cook for 6–7 minutes over a gentle heat until the vegetables soften. Add the tomato paste, wine and stock and simmer for 12–15 minutes. If necessary the soup may be thickened by mixing 25g/1oz plain flour with a little stock and adding it to the pan. Be careful to whisk continuously as you add the thickening agent. Taste and season. Garnish with parsley when serving.

This simple soup is made with fresh mushrooms. It is not blended, so the texture is rustic. Make use of the variety of mushrooms that are available, though I wouldn't use more than two or three different kinds.

Adding wine to food really helps to improve and intensify the flavour. You don't need to use an expensive wine, but don't use a cheap one either. Only use a wine that you would drink. Do ensure that you simmer – not boil – the wine to allow the alcohol to evaporate, leaving a subtle, interesting flavour.

A creamy soup that is low in fat and high in flavour. The roasting of the garlic gives the soup a sweet and mellow edge while the potatoes provide the creamy texture.

A wonderful source of seasoning in cooking, garlic is also widely recognised for its health-giving benefits. Studies show that garlic has beneficial uses and may help to lower cholesterol levels and reduce blood clotting. Garlic can be taken in the form of odourless capsules, which can be obtained from health food and chemist shops, but if you enjoy the taste of garlic use it as much as you can in your cooking.

roasted garlic and potato soup

serves 6

1– 2 heads garlic
2 dsp olive oil
1 large onion – finely chopped
freshly ground black pepper
2 good-sized potatoes – peeled and diced
570ml/1pt homemade chicken or
    vegetable stock
2 dsp parsley – coarsely chopped
1 bay leaf
4–6 spring onions – finely chopped

Sprinkle the whole heads of garlic with half of the olive oil and wrap them in tinfoil. Roast in the oven @ 200°C/gas mark 6 for approximately 30–45 minutes until the garlic has softened. Take the garlic out of the oven. You should now be able to squeeze it out easily from its papery skin.

Heat the remaining olive oil in a large saucepan and add the garlic and onion. Season with pepper. Cook over a gentle heat for 4–5 minutes until the onions become opaque. Now add the diced potatoes and cook for a further 2 minutes. Next, add the stock, parsley, bay leaf and spring onions and simmer gently for a further 45–60 minutes.

Allow the soup to cool slightly, remove the bay leaf, then whiz in a blender until the texture is smooth and creamy.

When you are ready to serve the soup, return it to the saucepan to warm it through. Check and adjust the seasoning as required. Serve the soup hot, garnished with crispy onions or spring onions.

green vegetable
soup with mint and yoghurt

serves 6–8

1 tsp olive oil
1 small onion – finely chopped
1 potato – peeled and diced
500g/1lb green vegetables – roughly chopped
570ml/1pt homemade light vegetable or
   chicken stock
freshly ground black pepper
good handful of fresh herbs, e.g. mint,
   basil, parsley, tarragon – roughly chopped
275ml/^{1}/2pt semi-skimmed milk
50g/2oz plain flour
natural yoghurt and herbs to garnish

A versatile soup recipe that be used with most green vegetables and can therefore be adapted to whatever vegetable is in season. Cooking times for vegetables will vary slightly. Vegetables such as spinach, asparagus, peas and beans will cook a lot more quickly than broccoli or fennel. Be careful not to overcook the soup or you will spoil the texture and colour.

Heat the oil in a large heavy-based pan and add the onion and potato. Cover and cook over a low heat for 4–5 minutes but do not allow the vegetables to brown. Add the prepared green vegetables and cook for 3–4 minutes until tender. Be careful not to overcook as this will spoil the colour of the vegetables. Add the stock and mix well. Taste and season with pepper and add the herbs.

Allow the soup to cool slightly, then place in a food processor and whiz until smooth. Return the soup to the pan and heat gently.

In a separate bowl, blend together the milk and flour until you have a smooth paste. Slowly add this to the soup, stirring continuously, and bring it to the boil. Simmer for 2 minutes, then serve immediately. Garnish with a swirl of yoghurt and a sprinkling of herbs.

corn and crab
chowder

1 dsp olive oil or butter
1 onion – diced
1 red pepper – diced
1 yellow pepper – diced
1 dsp spring onions – roughly
chopped
2 litres/4^1/4pt milk – low-fat or
full cream

25g/1oz flour
450g/1lb sweet corn – fresh or frozen
3–4 red potatoes – diced
pinch of freshly ground black pepper
450g/1lb fresh meat from crab claws
2 dsp whipping cream
1 dsp parsley or coriander

Heat the oil or butter in a large pan. Add the onion, peppers and
spring onions and cook gently for 4–5 minutes.

In a small bowl or cup mix a little of the milk with the flour to
form a paste and add it to the vegetables. Continue to cook the
vegetables over a low heat for another minute, then slowly add the
remainder of the milk, stirring well with each addition. Now, add
the potatoes, sweet corn and season. Simmer over a low heat for
15–20 minutes, but do not allow the vegetables to break down.

While the vegetables are simmering, prepare the crab. Crack open
the cooked claws and remove the flesh carefully. Break the meat
into even sized pieces and add to the soup five minutes before
serving.

When the soup is ready, garnish with a little cream and herbs.
Serve immediately.

This is a favourite
soup of mine, made
from fresh crab
meat. The claws
contain more meat
than the rest of the
crab and the meat
is also of a chunkier
texture and
therefore perfect
for a chowder. You
can buy cooked
crab claws in the
fishmonger's. It is
important that all
the vegetables are
diced to a similar
size.

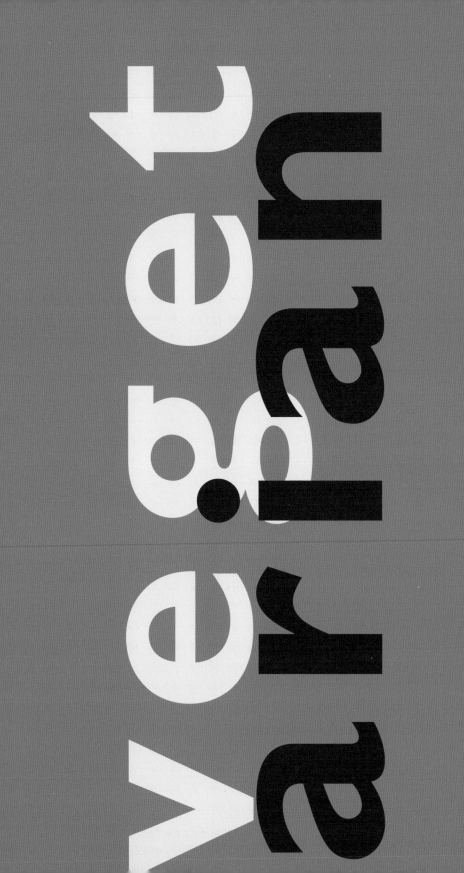

Eating **fresh** vegetables is essential if you want to stay healthy and well. Making full use of the huge variety of **vegetables** now available to us, the dishes in this section are strongly influenced by the flavours and aromas of the Mediterranean.

penne
pasta
with roasted tomato sauce

serves 4

Whether you buy it fresh or dried, pasta is the ultimate fast food. In this recipe, I've teamed it with a simple tomato sauce. The secret of this excellent sauce lies in the roasting of the tomatoes, which intensifies the sweet flavour.

450g/1lb cherry tomatoes
2–3 cloves garlic – finely chopped
2–3 chillies – finely chopped
1 dsp balsamic vinegar
2 dsp olive oil
1/2 onion – finely sliced

150ml/1/4pt water
1 dsp red pesto
penne pasta for 4
50g/2oz Parmesan
handful of fresh basil or flat-leaf parsley –
    coarsely chopped

Place the tomatoes, garlic and chillies on a baking sheet, sprinkle with balsamic vinegar and 1 dsp olive oil and grill or roast in a hot oven @ 200°C/gas mark 6 for 20–25 minutes. When cooked remove from the grill or oven and set to one side.

Heat 1 dsp olive oil in a shallow frying pan and add the onion. Cook for 2–3 minutes until softened and opaque. Now add the tomatoes, garlic, chillies and the water and simmer gently for 6–7 minutes. Add the pesto and cook for 4–5 minutes.

Serve the roasted tomato sauce over the pasta. Allow approximately 110g/4oz of pasta per person. Garnish with Parmesan and some basil or flat-leaf parsley.

A little goes a long way with pesto. A spoonful or two will spice up dressings and stews and, mixed with pasta, it makes a quick and tasty lunch or evening meal. What I really love about pesto is that it can be made in advance and will keep in the fridge for about a week.

basil
pesto

2 large handfuls basil
2 tsp garlic – crushed/finely chopped
2 tsp pine nuts
25g/1oz Parmesan – grated
2 dsp olive oil
juice of 1 lemon

Place all the ingredients in a blender or liquidiser. Blend until smooth. Season to taste. If you prefer, you can make your pesto using a pestle and mortar. This will give it a slightly coarser texture.

Pesto can be made with other green-leafed herbs and with other nuts. Try substituting walnuts for the pine nuts or replacing the basil with mint, rocket or coriander.

sauce for
summer salad
of pasta

2 dsp olive oil
1 tsp Dijon mustard
4 tbsp balsamic vinegar
2 tbsp hoisin sauce
1 inch root ginger – grated
1 tsp soft brown sugar

Place all the ingredients in a bowl or in a screw-top jar. Whisk or shake well. Serve over pasta and any other salad ingredients and toss well.

A fresh, light sauce that's ideal for a pasta salad.

creamy
coriander
sauce

50g/2oz pine nuts
1 good handful of coriander – finely chopped
1 tbsp olive oil
110g/4oz spring onions – finely chopped
225g/8oz low-fat cream cheese
150ml/^{1}/4pt milk
^{1}/2 tsp mustard
25g/1oz Parmesan – shaved

Mix two thirds of the pine nuts with two thirds of the coriander and mash to form a smooth paste. Using a pestle and mortar is the best way of doing this.

Heat the oil in a saucepan and add the spring onions. Cook gently for 1–2 minutes and add the cream cheese and the coriander and pine nut paste. Mix well and add the milk and mustard, stirring continuously. Finally add the remainder of the coriander and pine nuts and heat for a further minute.

Pour the sauce over the pasta and mix well. Sprinkle with shavings of Parmesan and serve at once.

This sauce goes well with pasta and is particularly good if you are having fish or chicken.

59

Noodles are quick, easy and versatile. They are ideal with sauces because they retain their individual texture but absorb other flavours very easily. Use whatever type of noodles you prefer.

thai
noodles
with pak choi and green vegetables

serves 4

the vegetables

Lightly oil a wok or a large non-stick pan. Add the spring onions, chillies and galangal or ginger. Cook for 2–3 minutes until they start to soften slightly. Now add the curry paste, mangetout, mushrooms and finally the pak choi. Mix well, then add the fish or soy sauce and coriander. Taste and season.

6 spring onions – roughly chopped
2 green chillies – deseeded and finely chopped
1 inch galangal or ginger – finely grated or chopped
1–2 tsp curry paste
175g/6oz mangetout – coarsely sliced
225g/8oz mushrooms – kept whole or halved, depending on size
3–4 pak choi – coarsely chopped
1–2 tsp fish sauce or soy sauce
1 dsp coriander – coarsely chopped
salt and freshly ground black pepper

the sauce

Mix the curry paste and yoghurt and drizzle over the vegetables. If you want to warm the sauce, add 25g/1oz cornflour mixed with 6 dsp water to the curry paste and yoghurt. Heat gently for 2 minutes.

4 tbsp thai curry paste
4 dsp Greek yoghurt or fromage frais

the noodles

When the sauce and vegetables are almost ready, cook the noodles by following the instructions on the packet. This should take approximately 3–4 minutes, though the finer noodles will cook more quickly. Place in a colander and drain twice under cold water. Reheat the noodles by pouring boiling water over them before serving.

To assemble the dish, arrange the noodles on plates and top with vegetables and sauce.

225g/8oz noodles – fine, medium, thick or flat

Galangal is from the same family as ginger and should be peeled and grated or chopped like ginger. Galangal is, however, slightly pinker and is more sour than hot in flavour.

This vegetarian frittata contains plenty of vegetables and protein. If you wish you can add salami or bacon bits. With a large bowl of salad or some spiced beans, this dish will serve more people.

ratatouille frittata

serves 3–4

Heat the oil in a large non-stick frying pan and add the onion and cook until softened.

Next add the pepper, courgette and tomatoes and continue cooking. Add the herbs, peas and sweet corn. Heat for a further 1–2 minutes.

- 2 dsp olive oil
- 1 onion – cut into slices
- 1 red pepper – thickly sliced
- 1 courgette – cut into chunks
- 2 tomatoes – cut into chunks
- handful parsley or basil – chopped or 1/2 tsp dried oregano
- 110g/4oz frozen peas
- 110g/4oz tinned sweet corn

In a separate bowl, beat the eggs and water. Season with black pepper. Pour the eggs over the vegetables in the pan and cook until the egg looks almost set. Layer or sprinkle the cheese on top of the frittata. Now place the pan below a hot grill for 2–3 minutes until the top of the frittata is golden and slightly risen. The frittata should slide easily from the pan. Garnish with parsley, cut into slices and serve on its own or with salad.

- 6 eggs
- 4 dsp cold water
- freshly ground black pepper
- 110g/4oz cheese, e.g. cheddar, goat's or Parmesan
- 1 dsp parsley – finely chopped

Eggs are a great source of protein and contain many important vitamins. They are, however, high in cholesterol, so it is a good idea to limit yourself to two or three week. Opt for free range eggs if you can – the chickens produce more nutritious eggs.

This comforting meal combines beans, bread, potatoes and a sprinkling of cheese. It can be spiced up with smoked sausage, bacon, or Tabasco sauce. If you feel the dish has too much carbohydrate then simply leave out the bread or potatoes – I like the combination and texture of both.

hot spiced
crusty bread
and beans

serves 3–4

Ensure that the chunks of potato are completely dry, and then place below a hot grill or on a grill pan for 4–5 minutes until they are crispy and golden. If you wish, you may sprinkle the potatoes with a little oil and paprika before cooking. When the potatoes are ready, place them in an ovenproof dish with the bread.

Mix together the beans, passata, mustard and paprika. If using sausage, cut into slices and add to the beans. Pour the mixture over the bread and potatoes and bake in the oven @ 200°C/gas mark 6 for 15–20 minutes.

Sprinkle with cheese just before serving.

4 large baked potatoes – cut into chunks
1 ciabatta bread or crusty loaf – sliced
1 dsp olive oil – optional
^{1}/2 tsp paprika – optional
400g/13oz tin baked beans
150ml/^{1}/4pt passata or tomato juice
1 tsp mustard
^{1}/2 tsp paprika – optional
110g/4oz spicy smoked sausage – optional
50g/2oz mozzarella or cheddar cheese

Risotto just has to be one of the tastiest dishes around. Not only does it make a great meal for dinner parties, but, because of the creamy texture of the rice, it's also the perfect comfort food. I've used green spring vegetables, such as asparagus and courgettes, to give this risotto freshness and colour.

spring vegetable risotto

Lightly steam the courgettes and asparagus for 2–3 minutes until tender. Set to one side.

Spray the pan with the oil. Add the spring onions and chilli and cook for 3–4 minutes. Add the lemon zest and rice and stir until the rice is well mixed and coated. Now add the wine and half of the stock and cook gently. Stir continuously until the stock is almost completely absorbed. Now add the courgettes and asparagus and a little more stock. Continue adding the stock, a little at a time, stirring frequently, until all the liquid has been absorbed. The risotto should now look quite creamy and the rice should be tender, though it should have some bite. If the rice is not cooked, add a little more stock and continue cooking. It should take approximately 10–12 minutes for all the stock to be absorbed and for the rice to cook.

When the rice is cooked, add the cream or yoghurt and parsley and season to taste. Serve with a sprinkling of freshly grated Parmesan.

1/2 tsp olive oil
4 dsp spring onions – finely chopped
1 green chilli – deseeded and finely
   chopped
275g/10oz risotto rice
zest of 2 lemons
150ml/1/4pt dry white wine
570ml/1pt light vegetable stock
1 courgette – diced
225g/8oz asparagus tips

1 dsp yoghurt or cream
1 dsp parsley – finely chopped
salt and freshly ground black pepper
25g/1oz freshly grated Parmesan

tip

If possible, use fresh stock in your risotto – it does make all the difference.

These kebabs are quick and easy and they taste fantastic. I've used lemon grass sticks instead of kebab sticks for a change. The lemon grass sticks will scent the kebabs with a gentle lemon flavour.

veggie
lemon grass
kebabs

This is a novel way to cook veggie mixture. A combination of chickpeas, beans and lentils can also be added and, if you want to spice it up, some herbs and paprika.

1 dsp oil
2 spring onions – roughly chopped
2 cloves garlic – finely chopped
1 inch ginger – finely grated
1 tsp turmeric
50g/2oz chickpeas – finely mashed
450g/1lb vegetarian sausages –
  skinned and mashed
1 egg – lightly beaten
6–8 lemon grass sticks

Heat the oil in a saucepan and add the spring onions, garlic, ginger and turmeric. Cook for 2–3 minutes. Add the chickpeas, sausage and egg and remove from the heat.

Stir well until the mixture begins to bind together. Form the mixture into bite-sized pieces and thread these onto lemon grass sticks. You should manage to get 3 or 4 pieces onto each stick. Place on the barbecue for approximately 7–8 minutes. Turn occasionally and, when cooked, serve with the oriental sauce on page 72.

spicy bean burgers

400g/14oz can cannellini beans
50g/2oz cooked lentils – finely
   mashed (optional)
1 courgette – peeled and grated
50g/2oz nuts, e.g. hazelnuts, walnuts
   or almonds – finely chopped
1 dsp olive oil
1 red chilli – finely chopped
1 onion – finely chopped
2 cloves garlic – finely chopped
2 tsp mild curry paste

175g/6oz breadcrumbs – can be
   gluten-free
2 eggs – well beaten
2 tsp parsley – finely chopped

Drain the cannellini beans and place them in a bowl. Add the lentils, if you wish, and mash well. Now add the courgettes and mixed nuts. Give everything a good mix and set to one side.

Heat the oil in a large saucepan and add the chilli, onion and garlic. Cook gently for 1–2 minutes, then add the curry paste, mix and cook for a further minute. Now, add the bean mixture to the pan, give a good stir and continue to cook for an additional 2 minutes.

Remove the saucepan from the heat and add half of the breadcrumbs, half of the eggs and all of the parsley and mix well until everything binds together.

Divide the mixture into 6–8 portions, shape these into burgers and coat well with the remaining egg and breadcrumbs. Place on a tray and refrigerate for 30 minutes to allow the burgers to firm up before cooking.

Cook on the barbecue over a medium heat for 8–10 minutes, turning occasionally. Serve immediately.

These spicy bean burgers are not just tasty, they're also packed with foods that are good for you. It is important that all the ingredients for the burgers are finely chopped. This will ensure that they bind together more easily and do not fall apart during cooking.

Sometimes known as the white kidney bean, cannellini beans are large white beans that are widely used in Italian cooking. Like most beans, they are high in protein and contain useful levels of iron and folate.

This dish could be cooked under an ordinary grill, but to see and taste it at its best you really need to cook it on the barbecue. Try to choose as colourful an array of vegetables as you can – that way they'll not only taste great, they'll also look great! A great veggie dish on its own.

mixed grill
with feta cheese, olives and bruschetta

serves 6–8

dressing

Make the dressing by mixing together the olive oil, lemon juice and half of the parsley.

150ml/¼pt olive oil
2 tbsp lemon juice
1 dsp flat-leaf parsley

the vegetables

Slice the top off the garlic; cut the fennel in half and blanch in boiling water for 2 minutes; slice the courgettes lengthways; cut the red onions into chunks; deseed and slice the chilli peppers; and steam the asparagus for 4–5 minutes. The aubergine will need a little more advance preparation. Slice it and sprinkle with salt. This helps to remove the bitter flavour. Leave for 10 minutes, then rinse and pat dry.

2 whole heads garlic
2 bulbs of fennel
4 large Portobello mushrooms
2 courgettes
2 red onions
2 chilli peppers
10–12 asparagus
1 aubergine

When the coals are hot start arranging the vegetables on the barbeque, starting with the ones that will take longer to cook, such as the garlic, onions and fennel. Sprinkle the vegetables with a little of the dressing and cook, turning occasionally. Arrange the remainder of the vegetables on the grill, finishing off with the asparagus and mushrooms, which will cook quickly.

When the vegetables are cooked, sprinkle with crumbled feta cheese and olives, and give each portion a drizzle of the dressing. Garnish with the remainder of the parsley.

110g/4oz olives
110g/4oz feta cheese

bruschetta

When all the vegetables are almost ready, slice the bread and toast on the grill. Rub with a clove of garlic and drizzle with a little olive oil. Serve immediately with the barbecued vegetables.

1 ciabatta bread or crusty loaf
clove of garlic
olive oil

spanish-style
potatoes
in a spicy tomato sauce

A quick tasty snack based on the Spanish tapas dish, *patatas bravas*. Ideal as an hors d'oeuvre.

potatoes

Peel the potatoes, cut into small cubes and pat dry. Place on a baking sheet, sprinkle with olive oil and bake in the oven @ 200°C/gas mark 6 for 50–60 minutes or until the potatoes are soft and golden.

900g/2lb potatoes
sprinkling of olive oil

spicy tomato sauce

Heat the olive oil in a pan and add the onion, pimento, tomatoes and sugar. Cook for 2–3 minutes. Add the bacon and cook for a further minute.

Pour the spicy tomato sauce over the potatoes. Sprinkle with mozzarella cheese and brown below a hot grill. Serve with cocktail sticks for spearing the potatoes.

1 tsp olive oil
1/2 onion – finely chopped
1–2 tsp pimento or sweet pepper sauce
375g/13oz tin chopped tomatoes
1 tsp sugar
50g/2oz bacon – cooked and roughly chopped
50g/2oz mozzarella – grated

roasted
garlic
and potato
purée

This tasty purée is an ideal accompaniment to the jewelled duck stew on page 92. Adjust the quantity of milk or cream depending on how creamy and smooth you want your mash.

Slice the top from the bulb of garlic. Place on a piece of tinfoil, sprinkle with olive oil, wrap and roast for 35–40 minutes, depending on the size of the garlic.

While the garlic is roasting, place the potatoes in a saucepan and boil in salted water for 15–20 minutes until tender. Drain and mash with milk or cream to give a light, creamy texture. Taste and season. Finally, remove the garlic from the oven, squeeze it out of its papery skin and mix it into the purée. Serve immediately.

1 head garlic
1 dsp olive oil
700g/1 1/2lb floury potatoes – peeled and diced
2–3 dsp milk or cream
salt and freshly ground black pepper

spicy parsnip mash

450g/1lb potatoes
450g/1lb parsnips
2 dsp low-fat milk – warmed
1 tsp paprika
1 tsp English mustard – optional
herbs to garnish

Peel the potatoes and cut into chunks. Boil for 15–20 minutes or until tender. Drain and mash.

Peel and slice the parsnips and place them in a separate pan. Steam for 12–15 minutes until the parsnips are tender. Drain and mash.

Mix the potatoes and parsnips in a large bowl and add the milk and paprika. If you want a little heat, add some English mustard too. Mix well and serve garnished with parsley or any seasonal herb.

Potatoes and parsnips make an excellent partnership, especially in mash. I've used some paprika to give this mash a bit of a kick!

sweet potato mash

1kg/2¼lb sweet potatoes
25g/1oz butter
juice of ½ lime
good pinch of freshly ground black pepper
1 dsp coriander – finely chopped
coriander to garnish – roughly chopped
lemon to garnish – cut into wedges

Scrub the sweet potatoes, prick with a fork and place on a baking sheet. Roast in the oven @ 200°C/gas mark 6 until tender. Cooking time will depend on the size of the potatoes, but it should take approximately 1¼ hours.

When the potatoes are cooked, remove from the oven, peel and mash in a warm bowl.

Add the butter, lime juice, black pepper and coriander. Mix well and serve garnished with more coriander and lemon wedges.

Sweet potatoes have a wonderful flavour that works very well with spiced dishes. The best way to cook them is to roast them in their skins. Delicious!

barbecue
mop-up
sauce

serves 4

1 dsp olive oil
1 onion – grated
2 stalks celery – finely chopped
150ml/^{1}/4pt tomato ketchup
4 dsp cider vinegar
150ml/^{1}/4pt water
1 vegetable stock cube
1 tsp cayenne pepper
75g/3oz soft brown sugar

Full-bodied and full of flavour. Barbecue food is perfect for mopping up this sauce!

Heat the oil in a small saucepan, add the onion and celery and cook for 2–3 minutes.

Add the remainder of the ingredients and simmer for 15–20 minutes.

This sauce can be made in advance and stored in the fridge for up to three days.

oriental-style
sauce

serves 6

150ml/^{1}/4pt plum sauce
150ml/^{1}/4pt hoisin sauce
2 dsp honey
1 tsp chilli sauce
1 dsp Worcestershire sauce
1 tsp sundried tomato paste

Hot, spicy, sweet and delicious, this sauce is ideal for dipping or pouring. It may be served hot or cold.

Place all the ingredients in a bowl and mix well. Store in the fridge and use within 48 hours.

baby onions
with a buttery
tarragon sauce

8–10 small onions
1 dsp olive oil

tarragon sauce

50g/2oz melted butter
4 dsp olive oil
1 tsp English mustard
salt and freshly ground black pepper
handful of tarragon – roughly chopped

Peel the onions, but do not chop off the base as you want
to ensure that the onions remain whole. Make a small cross
on the top of each onion – this will help them to cook –
then brush the onions with a little oil and place on the hot
barbecue. Cook until tender – approximately 30–40
minutes, depending on the size of the onions.

When the onions are almost cooked, place all the
ingredients for the sauce, except the tarragon, in a bowl and
whisk well. Pour into a saucepan and warm gently. Do not
boil. Remove from the heat, add the tarragon and mix.

Serve the onions piping hot. Drizzle with the buttery
tarragon sauce.

Baby onions are
delicious when
cooked on the
barbecue as they
become tender
and sweet. It's
worth noting,
however, that the
cooking time is
around 40 minutes.
Serve them piping
hot with this
delicious buttery
sauce.

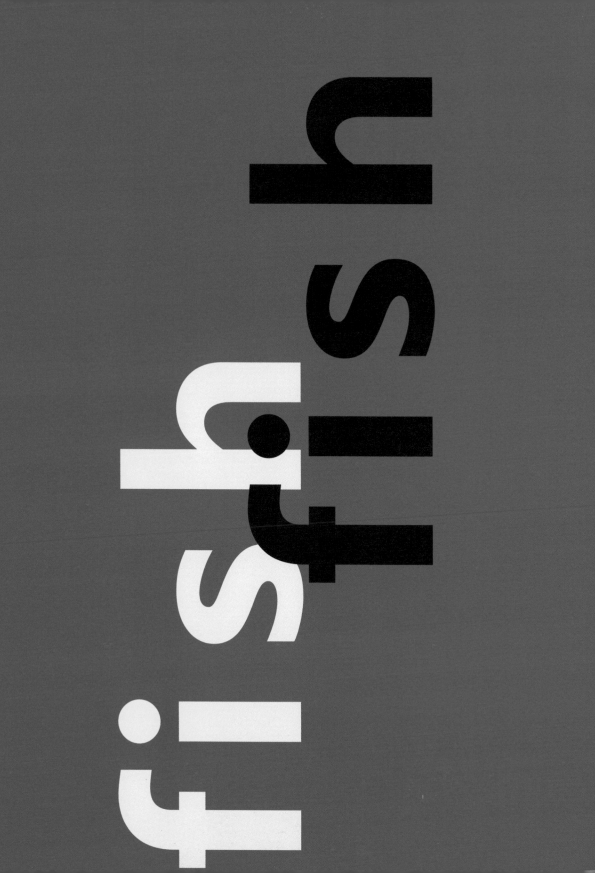

Surely one of the **healthiest, freshest** and most **delicious** foods around. **Keep it simple** – olive oil, a knob of butter and a twist of **lemon juice** will transform any fish – or try these more adventurous **paellas**, fish cakes and fiery sauces.

Paella is a wonderful dish, full of the colours and flavours of Spain. This recipe is for a basic paella that will suit vegetarians. As you'll see, though, I've added prawns and spicy sausage at the end. These are optional – feel free to add other kinds of seafood or chicken. This paella can be cooked on the hob, but I cooked this one on the barbecue – all you need is a large shallow pan with a heavy base.

paella

serves 6

Prepare all ingredients in advance and ensure the coals of the barbecue are not too hot.

Mix the saffron with hot water and leave to infuse for 10 minutes. If possible, try to use fresh stock, though vegetable stock cubes will do.

Pre-heat the paella pan or a large frying pan on the barbecue. Heat the oil, then add the onions and garlic and cook until opaque. Next add the peppers, courgettes, green beans and spring onions and cook for 2–3 minutes.

If prawns or sausage or any other meat or fish are being used, then place them on the barbecue at this stage and cook gently.

Now, gradually add the rice to the pan, stirring continuously as you do so to ensure that the rice is coated in the oil and flavours in the pan. This should take around 3 minutes. Next add the stock and saffron and allow the mixture to simmer gently until all the liquid has been absorbed and the rice is cooked. This should take approximately 10–12 minutes. Add the tomatoes, cayenne pepper and half of the herbs. Taste and season and cook for a further 2–3 minutes. Serve the paella immediately. Garnish with chunks of lemon, with the remainder of the herbs and with the prawns or sausage if you are using them.

1 tsp saffron threads
2 dsp hot water
1 dsp olive oil
1–2 onions – roughly chopped
2–3 cloves garlic – roughly chopped
1 red, 1 yellow, 1 orange pepper – diced
2 yellow or green courgettes – diced
225g/8oz green beans – sliced
6–8 spring onions – roughly chopped
450g/1lb long-grain rice
1.2 litres/2pt vegetable stock
6–8 ripe tomatoes – diced
2 tsp cayenne pepper
good handful of flat leaf parsley or basil
salt and freshly ground black pepper
2 lemons

optional

450g/1lb large prawns
450g/1lb spicy sausage, e.g. chorizo

yoghurt
baked fish

Any fresh firm white fish, such as haddock, monkfish, cod or whiting, can be used for this recipe. If possible, try to ensure that the fillets are of a similar size. This dish is very versatile and is ideal served with salad, pasta, rice or, as I do here, with a garlic and herb mash. The choice of herbs for both the fish and the potatoes can be varied depending on the season.

6 tbsp low-fat natural yoghurt
2 tbsp basil or parsley
2 tbsp sundried tomato paste or pesto or black olive paste
2–3 sundried tomatoes (optional) – finely sliced
1/2 tbsp dried oregano – optional
4 fish fillets – 175g/6oz each
1 lemon
handful of herbs

Make a sauce by mixing together the herbs, yoghurt and paste. A few slices of sundried tomatoes can also be added along with some dried oregano.

Place the fish in an ovenproof dish and pour the sauce on top. Grill or bake in the oven @ 200°C/gas mark 6 for approximately 20 minutes or until cooked.

Garnish with slices of lemon and herbs. Serve immediately.

garlic and herb mash
butterless and creamless

This is a tasty and healthy way to serve mashed potatoes. I've done away with the milk and butter and given the mash a more Mediterranean flavour by adding olive oil, herbs, garlic and crunchy red onion.

6–8 large potatoes – peeled and cut into chunks
1 tbsp olive oil
1 red onion – finely sliced
2 cloves garlic – finely chopped
1 dsp fresh herbs, e.g. parsley/basil

Cook the potatoes in boiling salted water for 15–20 minutes or until tender. Drain off the water and reserve a little of the liquid. Mash the potatoes well and cover to keep warm.

Place the olive oil, garlic and red onion in a small pan and cook until the onion and garlic begin to brown and become crispy. Add this mixture to the mashed potatoes along with a little of the reserved liquid. Mix well and serve garnished with herbs.

Mackerel is one of the tastiest oil-rich fish and is high in Omega 3 fatty acids. The potatoes and leeks, both low in cholesterol, are a perfect balance to the smoky flavour of the fish.

crunchy
mackerel
and potato galette

serves 4

Gently boil the potatoes for approximately 10 minutes. Be careful not to overcook them – you want them to be tender but still hold their shape.

Remove the skin from the mackerel and flake the fish into coarse chunks with a fork. Place it in a bowl and sprinkle with the lemon zest.

Warm a non-stick pan and add the leek, onion and spring onions and cook until softened and slightly golden. Add the sliced potatoes and cook very gently for a further minute. Again be careful to ensure that the potatoes hold their shape.

Spread three quarters of the potato, leek and onion mixture in the bottom of a 1.2 litre/2pt ovenproof dish. Top with the mackerel and then cover with the remainder of the potato and leek mixture.

In a large bowl, mix the yoghurt, fromage frais and milk. Pour it over potatoes and leeks, ensuring everything is well covered. Bake in the oven @ 190°C/gas mark 5 for 20–25 minutes until the top is crispy and golden. Garnish with parsley. Serve immediately with a fresh green salad.

450g/1lb potatoes – unpeeled and sliced
2 smoked mackerel fillets, peppered if you wish
zest of 1 lemon
1 leek – sliced
1 onion – sliced
1–2 spring onions

2 dsp low-fat yoghurt
2 dsp fromage frais
2–4 dsp low-fat milk
2 dsp parsley – coarsely chopped

Omega 3 is a polyunsaturated fatty acid and is essential to human health and growth. It is known to help prevent heart disease and cancer and helps to maintain a healthy nervous system. The best source of Omega 3 is fish – salmon, tuna and mackerel and other oil-rich fish are all good sources. If possible, try to eat at least two fish meals each week.

These lightly spiced cod cakes work extremely well with this sweet and fresh pineapple salsa. I've used cod for the fish cakes, but haddock, hake and other kinds of firm fish will work well too.

crispy
cod cakes
with green peppercorn, lime
and pineapple salsa

serves 4

Steaming and microwaving are two of the best and healthiest ways of cooking fish. Place the cod on a flat plate and pop in the microwave or place in a steamer for 3–4 minutes until the fish becomes tender and shows signs of flaking. Allow the fillets to cool, then flake into a bowl. Add the coconut, onion, breadcrumbs, cayenne or black pepper, chilli sauce and, finally, the egg. Mix well to bind the mixture together. Shape the mixture into rounds of approximately 5–7.5cm/2–3 inches and flatten to form fish cakes.

Heat the oil in a pan and add the fish cakes. Cook over a medium heat for 3–4 minutes on each side until golden brown. Place on kitchen paper to remove any residual oil and serve warm with pineapple salsa and rocket leaves.

450g/1lb cod fillets
50g/2oz shredded coconut flakes
1/2 small onion – finely chopped
50g/2oz fresh white breadcrumbs – can be gluten-free
1/2 tsp cayenne/black pepper
1/2 tsp chilli sauce
1 egg – lightly beaten
1 dsp olive oil

pineapple salsa

Mix all the ingredients together in a large bowl. Cover and chill in the fridge for 30 minutes before serving.

225g/8oz fresh pineapple – finely diced
1 tsp green peppercorns – crushed
juice of 1 lime
zest of 1/2 lemon
1 inch root ginger – grated
pinch of freshly ground black pepper
handful of coriander – finely chopped

This dish is simplicity itself – fish and leeks poached in saffron and white wine – and all the more delicious for it. You need at least two types of fish for this recipe, and ideally three. Cod, haddock, monkfish, trout and salmon all work well.

saffron-scented
fish medley

serves 4

Place the saffron threads in the water and leave to infuse for 10 minutes.

Skin the fillets and cut into bite-sized pieces.

In a shallow pan, heat together the white wine, milk, cream, butter, lemon zest, paprika, saffron threads and liquid, and the stock. Give this a good stir and add the fish and leek and poach gently over a low heat for approximately 4–5 minutes until tender. Do not stir while the fish is cooking. Instead shake the pan gently – this will prevent the fish breaking up. During cooking the sauce will thicken slightly.

10–12 saffron threads
2 dsp hot water
450g/1lb assorted fish
2–3 dsp white wine
150ml/¼pt milk
150ml/¼pt single cream
25g/1oz butter
zest of 1 lemon
¼ tsp paprika
4 dsp reduced fish stock
1 medium leek – finely sliced

scallion mash

Cook the potatoes in boiling salted water until soft and tender. Drain and mash. Cover to keep warm and set to one side.

In a small pan, heat together the butter, milk, pepper and spring onions for 1 minute. Add to the warm potatoes and mix well.

To assemble the dish, spoon the fish and its sauce into 4 individual bowls. Top with scallion mash and sprinkle with cheese. Flash below a hot grill until bubbling and golden. Garnish with parsley and serve immediately.

4–5 potatoes – peeled and diced
2 dsp scallions or spring onions – finely chopped
25g/1oz butter or sunflower oil
4 dsp low-fat milk
pinch freshly ground black pepper
25g/1oz cheddar – grated
1 dsp finely chopped parsley to garnish

seared crusted fish
with mustard, herby lentils and watercress

serves 4

450–700g/1–1¹/₂lb monkfish – cut in 1 large fillet
juice of 1 lemon
6–8 slices streaky bacon, prosciutto or Parma ham
1dsp olive oil

225g/8oz puy lentils
¹/₂ dsp olive oil
¹/₂ tsp mustard
2–4 dsp mixed herbs, e.g. basil, chives, flat leaf parsley
1 dsp spring onions – coarsely chopped
1 packet watercress – lightly steamed

Remove the skin from the fish if necessary and remove the central bone if you are using a cartilaginous fish. Clean the fish well. Sprinkle with some lemon juice, then wrap the fillets, either separately or together, in bacon or lightly smoked ham – unsalted bacon will have a milder flavour. Sprinkle with a little olive oil, place in a small roasting tin and cook for in the oven @ 190°C/gas mark 5 for approximately 20–25 minutes until the fish is tender and it can be easily flaked with a fork. The cooking time will depend on the size of the fish fillet. When the fish is cooked, turn the heat off but leave the fish in the oven to keep it warm.

To make the herby lentils

Following the instructions on the packet, place the lentils in a large saucepan and boil until they are tender. Drain and add the olive oil, mustard and spring onions and cook for a further minute. Finally, add the coarsely shredded herbs and serve at once.

Arrange the lentils on a bed of watercress and serve the fish fillets on top.

Monkfish is probably one of the easiest fish to cook, due to its firm flesh. An added advantage is that it is a cartilaginous fish and has only one central bone which is easy to remove. This dish can also be made with large fillets of salmon or any of the round white fish variety, such as cod or haddock. However, the texture needs to be robust. This dish also uses lightly smoked ham, such as Parma ham, or bacon, both of which can become quite salty during cooking, so be careful with the seasoning of this dish.

Meat is an important part of our diet and is **full of nutrients**. I've mostly used the healthier white meats such as chicken or turkey, but whether you fancy a lean lasagne or a jewelled duck stew, you're sure to find **a dish for every occasion**.

roasted
pork fillet
with tamarind chilli sauce

The tamarind in this dish gives a new twist to a Sunday lunch favourite. Of African origin, tamarind has a sour fruity taste that works very well with pork and complements the heat of the chillies. Often used in curries and Asian cooking and now readily available in most supermarkets, it will turn this sauce rich dark in colour. Serve this dish with the sweet potato mash on page 71.

If you prefer, substitute the tamarind paste with black bean, hot curry or even Thai paste.

Serves 6

1 dsp olive oil
2 green chillies – finely chopped
4 cloves garlic – finely chopped
50g/2oz soft brown sugar
150ml/^{1}/4pt vegetable stock
1 dsp Worcestershire sauce
good pinch of freshly ground black pepper
2 tbsp tamarind paste
2 dsp coriander – finely chopped
2 pork fillets – 700g/1 ^{1}/2lb each
coriander to garnish

Heat the oil in a saucepan. Add the chilli and garlic and cook for 2–3 minutes. Add the sugar and stock and stir until the sugar has dissolved. Now, add the Worcestershire sauce and the pepper and heat through for another minute. Next, add the tamarind paste, give the sauce a good stir and add the coriander. Stir again, bring the sauce to the boil and continue to simmer for 5 minutes.

Prepare the pork fillets by removing any excess fat. Tie the two fillets together and place on a large piece of foil. Pour the sauce over the pork and fold the foil around the pork to form a secure parcel. Place in a hot oven @ 190°C/gas mark 5 and roast for 1 ^{1}/4–1 ^{1}/2 hours until the pork is fully cooked. Baste occasionally.

Remove from the oven and garnish with finely chopped coriander. Serve immediately with sweet potato mash.

Lasagne is a great standby recipe. I've suggested three alternative toppings: a classic cheese sauce, a yoghurt-based sauce and one with Italian ricotta cheese and egg white for a crunchy topping.

lasagne

Serves 6–8

Place the lean beef in a non-stick pan and brown at a high temperature for 5–6 minutes to seal in the flavour. Add the balsamic vinegar, red onion, garlic and tomatoes and cook for 3–4 minutes. Add the lentils and stock and allow to simmer for 10–15 minutes to develop the flavour. Add the parsley for natural seasoning and remove from the heat.

Gently steam the spinach for 2 minutes and set to one side.

450–700g/1–1 1/2lb extra-lean minced beef
2 dsp balsamic vinegar
1 red onion – finely chopped
2 cloves garlic – finely chopped
225g/8oz cherry tomatoes
175g/6oz lentils – cooked
275ml/1/2pt homemade vegetable stock
2 dsp parsley
225g/8oz spinach

cheese topping

Place the milk and flour in a saucepan and bring to the boil, whisking thoroughly. Add the onion and cheese and mix well.

270ml/1/2pt low-fat milk
25g/1oz white flour
1 dsp onion – finely chopped
25g/1oz strong cheese, e.g. gorgonzola, Parmesan, mature cheddar

yoghurt topping

Mix all the ingredients together. It is important to use sheep's milk yoghurt, which is creamy and luxurious. The acidity and lack of body typical of low-fat yoghurt is not good for this sauce. Because it is very thin it does not hold its shape.

275ml/1/2pt sheep's milk yoghurt
2 dsp fromage frais
1 dsp finely chopped onion
pinch paprika pepper
1 egg
25g/1oz mature strong-flavoured cheese

ricotta topping

Beat the egg whites until stiff, fold in the cheese, milk, mustard, Tabasco and Parmesan

3 egg whites
150g/5oz ricotta cheese
150ml/1/4pt low-fat milk
1 tsp mustard
1 tsp Tabasco sauce
1 dsp Parmesan cheese

Place a layer of lasagne in the bottom of a rectangular ovenproof dish. Top with half of the meat mixture and half of the spinach. Add another layer of lasagne and repeat the process. Cover with the topping of your choice and bake in the oven at 200°C/ gas mark 6 for 25–30 minutes. Serve hot and golden.

6–8 sheets 'no cook' lasagne

beef
with bamboo shoots and noodles

450g/1lb chump or frying steak – very finely sliced
225g/8oz assorted mushrooms – fresh or dried
1 tsp oil
1 tsp root ginger – finely chopped or grated
1 tsp soy sauce
225g/8oz tin bamboo shoots
225g/8oz tin water chestnuts
110g/4oz spinach – shredded
6–8 spring onions – coarsely chopped
275ml/$^{1}/_{2}$pt beef stock
225g/8oz noodles

To slice the beef, place it in the freezer for 10 minutes to allow it to firm up. It should now slice easily.

Soak any dried mushrooms in a little warm stock for 10 minutes. Fresh mushrooms should be washed and sliced.

Heat the oil in a large saucepan and add the beef, ginger and soy sauce. Fry the meat for approximately 6–8 minutes until it is crispy and well cooked. Add the bamboo shoots, water chestnuts, spinach, spring onions and half of the stock. Simmer gently for 3–4 minutes.

Cook the noodles, following the instructions on the packet, and place in individual serving bowls. Cover with the beef and vegetable mixture and 2–3 dsp of the remaining stock.

Stir-frying is a quick and healthy method of cooking. Only a small amount of oil is used, and the short cooking time ensures that the vegetables have bite and do not lose their vitamin content.

This one-bowl lunch or dinner is ideal if you need to make something that's quick and easy. The assorted mushrooms may be dried or fresh or a combination of both. If possible, try to use fresh stock. I have only used a small amount of soy sauce because of its salt content.

potato and
bacon dahl

3–4 potatoes – thickly sliced
1 dsp olive oil
350g/12oz lentils or yellow split peas
1 tsp turmeric
1/2 tsp cumin
150ml/1/4pt vegetable stock
110g/4oz tinned sweet corn

1 dsp olive oil
1 onion – coarsely sliced
2–3 cloves garlic – finely chopped
6–8 rashers bacon
pinch of paprika
1 red chilli – finely chopped – or
1 tsp chilli paste

I love lentils. They are inexpensive, quick and easy to prepare, and full of goodness. They absorb flavours and spices extremely well and are a healthy and tasty alternative to potatoes or bread. Tinned lentils will work equally well in this recipe.

Lightly steam the sliced potatoes for 3–4 minutes until they are almost cooked. Sprinkle with olive oil and place in a grill pan or under a hot grill for 4–5 minutes until cooked and slightly blackened.

Place the lentils in a large saucepan with the turmeric, cumin and the stock and cook for 15–20 minutes until the lentils have softened and almost resemble a paste. Remove from the heat, mash gently and add the sweet corn.

In a separate pan, heat the olive oil and add the onion, garlic and bacon. Cook for 5 minutes until slightly blackened, then add the paprika and chilli. Mix well and continue cooking for a further 1–2 minutes.

To assemble the dish, add the griddled potatoes to the lentils, mix well and pour into a large serving dish. Top with the bacon and onions.

If necessary, a little water or stock may be needed to adjust the consistency.

Garnish with parsley or coriander and serve with sticky rice.

Lentils are a great health food. Low in fat and calories, they are high in iron, folic acid and protein. Lentils are also rich in fibre, and regular consumption can help to lower cholesterol levels.

italian
lamb stew
with lentils

2 lemons
900g/2lb lamb pieces – trimmed and cut into large chunks
6 dsp parsley (flat-leaf or curly) – roughly chopped
1 tsp chilli flakes
$1/2$ tsp fennel seeds
$1/2$ tsp cumin
1 dsp oil
2 dsp olive oil
275ml/$1/2$pt light vegetable stock
110g/4oz lentils
110g/4oz green olives

Roast the lemons in a hot oven or below a grill for 4–5 minutes until soft and blackened. Squeeze out the juice and set to one side.

Place the lamb pieces in a large bowl with the parsley, chilli flakes, fennel seeds, cumin, lemon juice, olives and oil. Give the mixture a good stir, cover with cling film and leave to marinate in the refrigerator for up to 24 hours. This is one of those dishes where the flavour really does improve the longer it is left to sit.

When the flavours have infused, place the olive oil in a large heavy-based pan. Add the lamb pieces to the hot pan and toss around for 4–5 minutes to brown and seal in the flavour. Depending on the size of your pan, you may need to add the lamb in batches to ensure that it browns properly. When all the lamb has browned, add the stock, cover and leave to simmer gently for 1 1/2 hours. At the end of this time, add the lentils and olives and continue to cook slowly for 15–20 minutes.

Serve immediately, garnished with parsley.

Lamb is a meat that absorbs flavour very well and, in this dish, I've used it with plenty of herbs, spices and lemon. The sweetness of the roasted lemons works a treat in this stew. You will need to start preparing this dish the day before you want to use it. Serve with couscous or pasta.

This is a stew for a special occasion. I prefer to make it with duck, but lamb or chicken also work very well. The nuts, pomegranates and lemon give the stew freshness and texture.

duck stew

Serves 5–6

4 Barbary duck breasts
175g/6oz almonds or walnuts
2–3 pomegranates
1–2 tsp olive oil
1 large onion – finely chopped
2–3 spring onions – roughly chopped
1/2 tsp turmeric
1/4 tsp cumin
275ml/1/2pt chicken stock
zest and juice of 2 lemons

In a blender or with a pestle and mortar, blend or pound the nuts until they become smooth. Set to one side.

Halve the pomegranates, scoop out the juice and seeds and set to one side. The seeds should be bright red in colour, an indication that the pomegranates are ripe.

Remove the skin, then cut the duck breasts into fine slices. In a large shallow pan, heat the olive oil and add the onion. Cook gently for 2–3 minutes. Add the duck pieces and continue cooking for 7–8 minutes. Now add the spring onions, turmeric, cumin and nuts and cook for a further 3–4 minutes. Add the stock, bring to the boil and simmer gently for 15 minutes.

Just before serving, add the juice and seeds from the pomegranate and the zest and juice from the lemons.

Serve with jasmine rice or the roasted garlic and potato purée on page 70.

Duck contains three times as much iron as chicken and is a good source of potassium, zinc and all the B vitamins.

A tasty recipe, full of summer flavours and
goodness, and made with a wonderful sauce.
The crunchy topping is made with
croutons and pine nuts.

summertime lemon and
thyme chicken

Serves 4–5

chicken stock

You need to make a good chicken stock for this sauce. Place the
chicken, onion, carrot, bay leaf and parsley in a large pan and add
the water. Cover and simmer gently for 1¼–1½ hours. Remove the
pan from the heat and set to one side to cool. When the stock has
cooled it should be easy to skim any fat from the top. Now strain
the stock and return it to the pan.

3–4 chicken thighs/wings/drumsticks
1 onion – thickly sliced
1 carrot – thickly sliced
1 bay leaf
1 bunch of parsley
1.2 litres/2pt water

For this recipe, add the low-fat chicken soup to the pan and bring
to the boil. Cook for one minute and then leave it to cool slightly.

425g/15oz tin low-fat chicken soup

the chicken

Place the chicken strips in a hot non-stick pan and sprinkle them
with soy sauce and black pepper. Cook over a high heat for 3–4
minutes, tossing regularly, until the chicken has absorbed all the
flavour of the soy sauce. Add the onion, asparagus and mushrooms
and continue cooking for 3–4 minutes. Transfer the chicken and
vegetables to an ovenproof dish approximately 20–23cm/8–9 inches
in diameter. Pour the sauce on top.

450g/1lb chicken – skinned and cut
   into strips
2 dsp soy sauce
freshly ground black pepper
1 onion – coarsely sliced
450g/1lb asparagus – lightly steamed
225g/8oz mushrooms – thinly sliced

the topping

Toast or deep fry the bread to make croutons. Place them, along
with the oil, zest, lemon thyme and pine nuts in a shallow pan and
cook for two minutes, stirring regularly. Sprinkle the mixture over
the top of the chicken and sauce. Bake in the oven at 190°C/gas
mark 5 for 30–35 minutes.

2 slices bread – cut into cubes
2 dsp olive oil
zest of 1 lemon
1 tsp lemon thyme
50g/2oz pine nuts

Serve with a crisp green salad.

lemon grass and
garlic chicken

700–900g/1¹/₂–2lb chicken joints (skinned if preferred)
8–10 small potatoes – peeled
1 onion – thickly sliced
375/13oz tin tomatoes
1 chicken stock cube
150ml/¹/₄pt water
2–3 stalks lemon grass – lightly bruised
2 cloves garlic – finely chopped
2 inches root ginger – grated
freshly ground black pepper
1 dsp olive oil
400g/14oz tin coconut milk
2 dsp parsley or coriander – finely chopped

Place all the ingredients in an ovenproof casserole dish, except the coconut milk and the stock cube. Mix the stock cube with the water and pour it over the chicken and vegetables. Give everything a good stir, then place the dish in the oven @ 200°C/gas mark 6 for 1¹/₂ hours. The dish may also be cooked on the hob – bring to the boil and simmer gently for 1¹/₂ hours. About 10–15 minutes before serving add the coconut milk and the parsley or coriander. Return the stew to the oven to complete the cooking time. Remove the lemon grass. Serve with warm crusty bread.

This simple one-pot chicken stew is bursting with flavour. The lemon grass and coconut bring the exotic aromas and tastes of Thailand to the dish, while the potatoes give it that hearty warmth that is so comforting in cold wintry weather. Chicken thighs, drumsticks or wings can be used in this dish.

Chicken is relatively low in fat if eaten without the skin. It contains all the B vitamins, potassium and some iron.

middle-eastern saffron
chicken

4 cloves garlic – crushed
2 tsp cinnamon powder
1 tsp ground ginger
juice of 1 lemon
6 chicken fillets – skinned
1 onion – coarsely sliced
700g/1 1/2lb tomatoes – coarsely chopped
570ml/1pt light vegetable stock
1 tsp saffron threads
4 dsp hot water
2 tbsp honey
flat-leaf parsley – roughly chopped

This chicken dish is low in fat and very tasty. It is flavoured with spices and with the fresh, sweet flavour of tomatoes. The slightly bitter taste of saffron helps to balance the dish and also gives it its intense colour.

Mix the garlic, cinnamon and ginger with the lemon juice and use the mixture to coat the chicken fillets. Cover well and leave to marinate for at least 30 minutes.

Heat a non-stick pan until hot, then add the chicken fillets and cook on both sides for a total of approximately 4–5 minutes until the chicken just begins to colour. Add the onion, tomatoes and stock and simmer gently for 25–30 minutes until the chicken is tender and the onions have reduced down. Now, add the saffron and its liquid – the saffron threads should be placed in a small bowl with the hot water and left to sit for 10 minutes before using. Give the chicken a good stir and add the honey. If the sauce is too thick, add a little more stock until it reaches the consistency you desire. Garnish with flat-leaf parsley and serve immediately with couscous or rice.

This tasty dish, made with Parmesan, basil and ricotta, brings together some fantastic Italian flavours. It can be made a few hours in advance and simply popped into the oven when you are ready to eat.

pasta shells
with chicken and ricotta

Serves 6

tomato sauce

Place the oil, onion, tomato paste and fresh tomato in a saucepan and bring to the boil. Simmer gently for 15 minutes. Add a pinch of sugar to taste.

1 dsp oil
1 red onion – coarsely chopped
2 dsp sundried tomato paste
450g/1lb fresh tomatoes – chopped

cheese sauce

Place the oil and flour in a saucepan and heat gently for 2–3 minutes, stirring continuously. Add the milk and wine, whisk well and bring to the boil. Continue boiling for 1 minute. Add the cheese and paprika, mix well and leave to cool slightly.

1 dsp olive oil
25g/1oz plain flour
275ml/$^{1}/_{2}$pt low-fat milk
150ml/$^{1}/_{4}$pt dry white wine
25g/1oz Parmesan cheese – coarsely grated
pinch paprika

filling

Lightly steam the chicken in a steamer for 6–8 minutes until cooked. Place in a bowl and mix with the basil, egg and ricotta. Season with freshly ground black pepper. Leave the mixture to cool, then use it to stuff the lightly cooked pasta shells.

225g/8oz skinless chicken fillets – finely sliced
bunch basil leaves – coarsely chopped
1 egg – lightly beaten
110g/4oz ricotta
pinch sea salt and of freshly ground black pepper

350g/12oz large pasta shells – lightly steamed or boiled for 3 minutes

To assemble the dish, pour the tomato sauce into the base of a large ovenproof serving dish. Arrange the filled pasta shells on top and season well with just a pinch of salt and a good grinding of black pepper. Pour the cheese sauce over the pasta and bake in the oven @ 180°C/gas mark 4 for 15–20 minutes. If you wish, a little extra Parmesan can be scattered over the dish before baking. This will turn the top brown and crunchy. Serve on its own or with salad or warm granary bread.

tasty
turkey burger
with cherry tomato and mangetout salad

450g/1lb turkey mince
2 tbsp sundried tomato paste
1 tsp olive oil
1 onion – finely sliced
2 cloves garlic – grated
1 tsp chilli sauce
1 egg – lightly beaten
1 dsp soy or Worcestershire sauce
1–2 dsp parsley or thyme – chopped

275g/10oz cherry tomatoes – halved
175g/6oz mangetout
4 dsp extra virgin olive oil
2 cloves garlic – grated
zest and juice of 1 lemon

turkey burgers

Place the mince and tomato paste in a bowl and mix well. Don't rush this – you need to take time to bring the flavours together.

Heat the oil in a frying pan and add the onions, garlic and chilli sauce. Cook, stirring occasionally, for 5 minutes. Add this mixture to the bowl with the turkey and mix well. Leave to cool.

Add the egg, soy sauce and herbs to the turkey. Mix well to ensure that everything binds together. Divide the mixture and shape into 4 large or 8 small burgers. Cook on a baking sheet @ 200°C/gas mark 6 for 18–20 minutes or below a hot grill for 10–12 minutes. Serve hot with the tomato and mangetout salad.

cherry tomato and mangetout salad

Steam the mangetout for 1–2 minutes. Drain and place in large bowl with the tomatoes.

Make the dressing by placing the olive oil, garlic and lemon in a bowl and whisking well. Pour the dressing over the salad and serve at once.

These turkey burgers are ideal served in burger buns or can be served with salad or some other accompaniment. I've opted to make these burgers with turkey since this meat is low in fat and high in protein.

desserts

I simply couldn't do without **desserts** and you shouldn't either! There's a fantastic range here – from the **sheer indulgence** of marbled **chocolate** torte to healthier, fruit-based desserts, ice creams and sorbets. **Enjoy!**

sliced spiced
apple cake
with mango yoghurt

Serves 6

This is my low-fat alternative to traditional apple pie – spiced slices of apple baked in a delicious egg custard. When cooked, the custard sets around the apples so that it can be cut into wedges and served like a cake. This dish can be served on its own but is delicious if served with fromage frais or with mango yoghurt.

Mango pulp is a relatively new product – it is simply the puréed pulp of the mango. It comes in tins and can be found in Asian supermarkets.

Peel and core the apples and cut them into wedges. Place them in a bowl of water and add a squeeze of lemon juice. This will prevent the apples from turning brown.

In a separate bowl mix the flour, sugar, eggs and ground spices until smooth. Slowly pour in the milk and mix well. Transfer the mixture to a saucepan and heat gently for 2–3 minutes. Do not allow to boil.

When the mixture begins to thicken remove the saucepan from the heat and set it to one side to cool. Arrange the apples in a greased baking tin approximately 15–17cm/ 6–7 inches in diameter. Pour the custard over the apples and bake in the oven @ 200°C/gas mark 6 for 25–30 minutes until the apples have softened and the custard set. Serve sprinkled with a little vanilla-flavoured caster sugar or dust with icing sugar.

4–6 Bramley apples
juice of 1 lemon
50g/2oz plain flour
25g/1oz caster sugar
3 large eggs
1/2 tsp ground nutmeg
1/2 tsp ground ginger or cinnamon
275ml/1/2pt low-fat milk

mango yoghurt

Mix the ingredients together in a large bowl. Pour into a saucepan and warm gently for a few minutes. Do not boil. Serve with the sliced spiced apple cake.

150ml/1/4pt mango pulp
150ml/1/4pt fromage frais or
    natural yoghurt
1 tsp honey

cinnamon-spiced pear
crumble
with honeyed yoghurt

Serves 4

This quick and easy pudding is equally good with fresh or tinned pears. Add some dried fruits to the crunchy muesli topping to give added texture and interest.

Place the drained tinned or fresh pears in an ovenproof dish. If you are using tinned pears mix some of the tinned pear juice with the cinnamon and pour over the pears. If you are using fresh pears, mix the water, sugar and cinnamon and pour this over the pears.

2 x 375g/13oz tins pears or 6 pears – peeled, cored and quartered
2–3 dsp pear juice
2 dsp water
25g/1oz caster sugar
1/2 tsp cinnamon

muesli crumble

Place the dried fruits in a separate bowl and pour over the pear or orange juice. Leave for 15 minutes until the fruits begin to plump up.

Mix together the muesli and the polyunsaturated fat. Add the demerara sugar and the dried fruits. Mix well, then spoon the crumble over the pears. Bake in the oven @ 190°C/gas mark 5 for 20–25 minutes until the top is crunchy and golden.

50g/2oz dried apricots, raisins, sultanas
2–3 dsp pear or orange juice
175g/6oz crunchy muesli – low in sugar and salt
50g/2oz polyunsaturated fat
25g/1oz demerara sugar

honeyed yoghurt

Mix the yoghurt with the honey and serve with the crumble. Dust the yoghurt with a little cinnamon just before serving.

150ml/1/4pt Greek yoghurt
1 dsp honey
cinnamon for dusting

banana tiramisu

110g/4oz Mascarpone cheese
110g/4oz low-fat yoghurt or
  whipped cream
2–3 drops vanilla essence
110g/4oz sponge or Madeira cake
4–6 dsp demerara dark rum

4 bananas – sliced
zest and juice of 1 lemon
25g/1oz demerara sugar
lemon zest and mint to garnish

Serves 6

In a large bowl mix together the Mascarpone and the yoghurt or cream. Add the vanilla essence and mix well.

Cut the sponge into chunks and sprinkle with rum.

Place the bananas in a bowl and mix lightly with the lemon juice and zest and the sugar.

Choose a round serving dish, approximately 15–18cm/6–7 inches in diameter, and spread half of the Mascarpone mixture over the base. Now take half of the sponge and use it to form a layer and top with half of the bananas. Repeat the process with the remaining sponge and bananas. Cover the dish with cling film and chill in the fridge for 2 hours. Sprinkle with lemon zest and garnish with mint before serving.

This is my rather low-fat version of a classic. I love the flavour of bananas in this pudding. Choose ones that are ripe and sweet.

chargrilled banana
and pineapple wedges with a creamy butterscotch sauce

Serves 2–4

Place the bananas and pineapple in a large bowl. Add the juice, zest and sugar and mix gently. Place the fruit on the barbeque or on a grill pan until it begins to soften and blacken.

4 bananas – halved
1 pineapple – cut into chunky
  wedges
zest and juice of 1 lemon
zest and juice of 1 lime
25g/1oz demerara sugar

creamy butterscotch sauce

Heat the butter and sugar in a small saucepan. Bring to the boil and simmer until golden and bubbling. Add the cinnamon. Remove from the heat and allow to cool slightly. Stir in the yoghurt. Serve with chargrilled banana and pineapples and garnish with mint.

50g/2oz butter
50g/2oz soft brown sugar
pinch cinnamon
150ml/^{1}/4pt Greek yoghurt
mint to garnish

Fresh fruit at its best, cut into large chunky wedges. Serve with ice cream or yoghurt or with this delicious creamy butterscotch sauce.

105

Filo pastry is convenient to use and is very low in fat. It can be found in the freezer compartment of your supermarket and should be defrosted before use. I've used cherries as a topping for this tart but you can substitute a seasonal fruit of your choice.

cherry
tart

Serves 8–10

the topping

Place the cherries in a large saucepan with the sugar and water and poach very gently for 2 minutes until they show signs of beginning to soften. Do not allow the cherries to lose their shape. Mix the arrowroot with the water and add it to the cherries. Cook until the arrowroot turns to a clear glaze, then remove the saucepan from the heat and set to one side to allow the cherries to cool.

225–450g/8–16oz fresh cherries
25g/1oz caster sugar
125ml/4floz water
1 dsp arrowroot
2 dsp cold water

vanilla cream filling

Dissolve the lemon jelly in the boiling water. In a large bowl mix together the custard, vanilla essence, cream cheese, lemon zest and jelly. Place the bowl in the fridge for 15 minutes to chill the mixture. Do not allow to set completely.

6 cubes of lemon jelly
4 dsp boiling water
125ml/4floz custard
1/2 tsp vanilla essence
340–450g/12–16oz low-fat cream
    cheese
zest of 1 lemon

filo pastry case

Place the egg white in a bowl with the oil and lightly whisk. Brush each layer of the filo pastry with the egg-white mixture, layering a greased loose-bottomed round (20cm/8 inch) or rectangular (20 x 15cm/8 x 6 inch) tin. Trim off the excess pastry. Bake in the oven @ 190°C/gas mark 5 for approximately 15 minutes. When cooked, remove from the oven and leave to cool.

1 egg white
1 dsp sunflower oil
4–5 layers filo pastry

To assemble the dish, remove the pastry from the tin and place on a large serving dish. Spread the vanilla cream over the bottom of the case and decorate with the cherries. Place in the fridge for 30 minutes to chill.

Cherries contain useful amounts of vitamin C, and fresh cherries are a good source of potassium, which helps stabilise heartbeat and keeps the skin healthy.

A quick and convenient pudding made with meringues, yoghurt, chocolate sauce and almonds. Do adapt this recipe to suit yourself. I often cut down on the quantity of meringues and add some frozen yoghurt or ice-cream.

There is a great assortment of ready-made sauces today and many of them are very good. However, read labels very carefully to check the ingredients and the sugar and fat content. It is easy to make your own coulis. Simply mix 110g/4oz soft-berried fruit and 25g/1oz icing sugar and pass the mixture through a sieve.

Meringues are great for desserts if you're keeping an eye on the fat content of your food – egg whites, a main ingredient in meringues, are very low in fat.

quick meringue
pudding

Serves 4

2 packets meringues or approximately
   20 dessert meringues
275ml/$\frac{1}{2}$pt low-fat yoghurt
175g/6oz fresh fruit
150ml/$\frac{1}{4}$pt chocolate sauce or fruit coulis
50g/2oz toasted almonds
sprigs of mint for decoration

Break the meringues into chunks and mix with the low-fat yoghurt to lightly coat them. Now spoon the meringues into individual glasses until they are about half full. Spoon in some fresh fruit and top with more of the meringue mixture to fill the glasses. To finish off, squeeze a little chocolate sauce or fruit coulis over the top and decorate with toasted almonds, the remainder of the fruit and a sprig of mint.

I've teamed this crunchy ginger meringue with fruit and with the exotic and delicate perfumes of cardamom and orange-flower water. Orange-flower water is available in chemists, specialist shops and some supermarkets.

crunchy ginger
meringue
with peaches, nectarines and apricots scented with cardamom

Serves 4

the meringue

Beat the egg whites in a large bowl until stiff, then add half of the caster sugar. Beat well until stiff, then add the remainder of the sugar (white and brown), cornflour and orange-flower water. Beat the mixture again until stiff.

3 egg whites
110g/4oz caster sugar
25g/1oz soft brown sugar
2 tsp cornflour
2 tsp orange-flower water

Line two baking sheets with greaseproof paper and use two plates that are 23cm/9 inches and 15cm/6 inches in diameter to trace an outline. Transfer the mixture to the baking sheets, flatten out and, with a palette knife, form into the shape of the circles. Bake in the oven @ 150°C/gas mark 2 for 1 1/4 hours until the meringue is cooked. Remove from the oven and leave to one side to cool before gently removing the greaseproof paper from the bottoms.

to decorate

Stone the fruit, cut into chunks and place in a large bowl. Shell the cardamom pods and discard the outer casings. Crush the seeds, sprinkle them over the fruit and let the flavours infuse for approximately 10 minutes.

4 apricots
4 nectarines
4 peaches or 2 mangoes
2 kiwi fruit – peeled
4 cardamom pods – seeds only
275ml/1/2pt low-fat fromage frais
2 tsp honey
sprigs of mint

Mix half of the fromage frais with the honey and gently spread it over the larger of the cooled meringues. Now spread half of the fruit over the fromage frais. Place the second meringue on top of the fruit to create a sandwich effect, then decorate it in the same way with the remaining fromage frais and fruit. Garnish with some sprigs of mint.

This passion fruit dessert has an exotic feel that makes it ideal for dinner parties and special occasions. You will need moulds for this dessert.

passion fruit
mousse
with a tangy lime syrup

mousse

Place the sugar and water in a large saucepan and boil for approximately 6–7 minutes until the mixture takes on a syrupy consistency, but do not allow it to take on a brown colour. Take the saucepan off the heat and set to one side for a moment.

Beat the egg whites until stiff, then whisk continuously as you add them to the sugar syrup. Set to one side.

Cut the passion fruits in half and scrape the seeds and juice into a large bowl.

Place the warm water in a bowl and sprinkle the gelatine on top. Place the bowl in a pan of hot water for 2–3 minutes until the gelatine dissolves. Remove the bowl from the pan.

Stir a spoonful of the passion fruit into the gelatine. Add this to the rest of the passion fruit, then add the cream and/or yoghurt and mix well. Finally, fold in the egg-white syrup. Pour the mixture into four individual moulds, approximately 5–7.5cm/2–3 inches in diameter, and chill in the fridge for at least 1 hour until set and firm.

110g/4oz caster sugar
150ml/^{1}/4 pt water
2 small egg whites
6–8 passion fruits
12^1/2g/^{1}/2oz gelatine
2 dsp warm water
150ml/^{1}/4pt whipping cream or
    ^{1}/2 yoghurt and ^{1}/2 whipping cream

tangy lime syrup

Place the water and sugar in a large saucepan. Heat, stirring continuously, until all the sugar has dissolved. Mix the arrowroot with with the water and add it, along with the lime juice, to the saucepan. Bring to the boil and simmer for 1 minute.

To assemble the dessert, unmould the individual servings of passion fruit mousse and place on a dessert plate. They should come out easily but if you are finding it difficult simply place the moulds in a basin of warm water for 30 seconds, then turn them upside down onto the serving plate and the moulds should come away easily. Drizzle the mousse generously with tangy lime syrup and serve.

150ml/^{1}/4pt water
50g/2oz caster sugar
juice of 3 limes
25g/1oz arrowroot
1dsp water

quick brown bread
ice cream

Serves 4

225g/8oz brown breadcrumbs – can be
  gluten-free
150g/5oz soft brown sugar
275ml/^{1}/2pt whipping cream/yoghurt –
  mixed
150ml/^{1}/4pt custard

Ideal on its own
or as an
accompaniment to
fruit or cheesecake,
this ice cream is
good with the
chargrilled bananas
and pineapple on
page 105 or with
the caramel and
coconut sauce on
page 122.

Make the bread into breadcrumbs – this is easier if you
just pop the bread in a food processor. It also helps if the
bread is at least a day old. Place the breadcrumbs in a large
bowl.

Sprinkle the sugar onto a baking sheet and place under a
hot grill until the sugar just begins to melt and bubble.
Pour the sugar over the breadcrumbs and mix well. Add
the cream/yoghurt and custard and give the mixture
another good stir. Transfer the mixture to individual
moulds and place in the freezer until firm and set. This will
take 1–2 hours, depending on your freezer.

winter berry
cheesecake

50g/2oz butter or polyunsaturated fat
175g/6oz muesli
110g/4oz blackberries
110g/4oz blueberries
110g/4oz damson or victoria plums
2 dsp water
25g/1oz icing sugar
25g/1oz cornflour
125ml/4floz water
250g/9oz light cream cheese
25g/1oz icing sugar
1/2 tsp cardamom seeds – crushed
275ml/1/2pt yoghurt or whippping cream
or 1/2 and 1/2

the base

Place the muesli on a baking sheet and bake in the oven at 200°C/gas mark 6 for 4–5 minutes. Alternatively, toast the muesli under a hot grill for 1–2 minutes. Warming the muesli in this way will help to intensify the flavours.

Melt the butter in a small saucepan, then add the warmed muesli. Mix well until the muesli shows signs of sticking together, then transfer to a lined loose-bottomed tin, 18–20cm/7–8 inches in diameter. Press down well and leave to cool.

the topping

Wash the berries and stone and wash the plums. Place the fruit in a pan with the water and icing sugar and poach very gently for 1 minute. Remove half of the fruit from the pan and set to one side. Now mix the cornflour with the water and add it to the pan. Heat for another minute until the cornflour thickens and the glaze becomes clear. Leave to cool.

Beat the cream until stiff and then add yoghurt, if using. In a separate bowl, cream the icing sugar and the cream cheese until soft. Add the cardamom seeds, then fold in the cream/yoghurt mixture and mix well. Finally fold in the cooked fruit that was removed from the pan and set to one side. Now spread the cream and fruit mixture on top of the muesli base and place in the fridge for approximately 1 hour. When the topping has set remove the cheesecake from the tin and decorate with the cooled thickened fruits from the pan.

Serve with yoghurt or ice cream.

This very simple cheesecake can be made with a variety of healthier products – polyunsaturated fat instead of butter, low-fat cream cheese, and yoghurt instead of whipping cream. Also, a variety of gluten-free muesli products suitable for coeliacs can be found in many supermarkets. Diabetes sufferers can either reduce or leave out the sugar used in poaching the fruit and creaming the cheese.

Champagne, sorbet and red berries –
this stunning dessert is sheer indulgence!

red berry
sparkling red berry **sorbet**

Red fruit sorbet

Make a sugar syrup by placing the sugar and water in a heavy-based saucepan and boiling for approximately 2–3 minutes. Do not allow the mixture to brown. Set the mixture to one side to cool slightly, then add the lemon juice.

After removing their stalks, wash the strawberries and dry them well. Place them in a blender and whiz until smooth – be careful not to whiz too much as the colour of the fruit may spoil. Add the puréed fruit to the sugar syrup and mix until smooth. If you would like a particularly smooth sorbet, pass the mixture through a sieve to remove any seeds, but this is not really necessary. The sorbet may now be frozen in an ice-cream maker. Alternatively, place the sorbet in a large, shallow plastic container and place it in the coolest part of the freezer for around 2–3 hours until firm and frozen. Setting time will depend on the setting temperature of your freezer. Stir the mixture frequently during the freezing process to prevent ice crystal formation.

425ml/^{3}/4pt water
250g/9oz caster sugar
juice of 1 lemon
775g/1^1/2lb strawberries

sparkling berries

Wash the berries and remove any stalks. Now place the berries in a bowl and sprinkle with the caster sugar. Leave for 10 minutes, then pour champagne or sparkling wine over the berries.

To serve, place a scoop of sorbet in a tall, stemmed glass. Now pour in some of the berries and champagne. Garnish with mint.

775g/1^3/4lb berries, e.g. red currants,
   strawberries, raspberries or blueberries
2 tsp caster sugar
275ml/^{1}/2pt sparkling wine/champagne
mint leaves

summer berry
pudding
with a burnt toffee crust

Serves 6–8

700g/1 1/2lb soft fruits, e.g. raspberries,
strawberries, blackberries
zest and juice of 1/2 orange & 1/2 lemon
25g/1oz caster sugar

150ml/1/4pt low-fat yoghurt
150ml/1/4pt fromage frais
1 tsp rose water
25g/1oz demerara sugar
1 tsp icing sugar
mint leaves and redcurrants

the berries

Only wash the berries if really necessary as this causes them to
weep and lose colour. Halve any of the bigger strawberries. Place
the berries in a large bowl and sprinkle with the zest and juice of
the orange and lemon and with the caster sugar. If the berries are
sweet and ripe you may not need the sugar to sweeten the fruit.
Mix well and leave to sit for 30 minutes to allow the flavours to
combine.

the burnt toffee crust

In a large bowl mix the low-fat yoghurt and fromage frais. Add the
rose water and mix again. Place the berries in a shallow ovenproof
dish and cover with the yoghurt mixture. Ensure that the cream
reaches the edges of the dish so that the fruit is sealed
underneath. Sprinkle with demerara sugar and icing sugar and
leave for at least one hour. Sprinkle with 1 dsp of water just
before browning as this helps melt the sugar and speeds up the
caramelising process. When you are almost ready to eat, place the
fruits under a very hot pre-heated grill for 2–3 minutes until the
top is golden, toffee-like and crusted. Alternatively, use a cook's
blow torch to create the toffee crust. Garnish with mint and
redcurrants.

This pudding is
delicious – prime
summer berries
marinated in
orange and lemon
syrup and topped
with a burnt toffee
crust. The intense
flavour of the rose
water works very
well with summer
berries. It is
available in most
supermarkets and
is handy to have in
your cupboard for
flavouring desserts
like this.

This is a set chocolate torte made without a base and served with a delicious marbled topping which can be flavoured with chocolate, toffee or coffee. If you prefer a lower calorie version, then simply top the torte with yoghurt and fresh raspberries.

marbled chocolate
torte
with white chocolate marshmallow sauce

Serves 4

Place the chocolate pieces in a large bowl over a pan of hot water. Ensure that the pieces are small as this will prevent over-heating and spoiling of the chocolate during the melting process.

When the chocolate has completely melted, add the cream and the maple syrup and mix well. Turn off the heat but leave the bowl over the water to prevent the chocolate from hardening. Be careful not to overheat or the mixture will set.

450g/1lb good quality dark chocolate with at least 70% cocoa content – broken into small pieces
4 dsp whipping cream – lightly beaten
1 tsp maple syrup

the filling

If you are using cream, beat it until it forms soft peaks. Yoghurt or fromage frais needs only a quick mix. Do not use a thin yoghurt for this recipe – a firmer set yoghurt such as Greek yoghurt works much better.

Spoon the chocolate mixture into the bowl with the cream or yoghurt and add the cinammon, nuts and coffee. Mix well, then transfer to a lined loose-bottomed tin 15–17cm/ 6–7 inches in diameter. Place the torte in the fridge to set for approximately 4–5 hours.

570ml/1pt cream/yoghurt/fromage frais or any combination of all three
1 tsp ground cinnamon
50g/2oz pecan nuts – finely chopped
2 dsp Camp coffee – a type of liquid coffee that contains chicory

white chocolate marshmallow sauce

Place the chocolate and cream in a small bowl and set it over a saucepan of hot water until the chocolate melts. Mix well. Add the chopped marshmallows and heat for approximately 15–30 seconds until they show signs of softening. Be careful not to overheat – the sauce only needs to be warmed. Drizzle the sauce over the chilled chocolate torte to create a dazzling marbled effect.

225g/8oz white chocolate – broken into small pieces
125ml/^{1}/4pt whipping cream
50g/2oz chopped marshmallows

nutty lemon and
ginger cake

If you wish to prepare a gluten-free cake, simply use gluten-free baking powder and gluten-free plain flour. These products are now available in most supermarkets.

This cake has a lovely texture and much of the flour is replaced with coconut, almonds and polenta. You can use a round or a square tin for this cake, or even a muffin tin to make individual muffins.

175g/6oz unsalted butter – softened – or polyunsaturated fat
175g/6oz caster sugar
1 tsp baking powder
75g/3oz polenta
50g/2oz plain flour
3 small eggs – lightly beaten

75g/3oz dessicated coconut
110g/4oz ground almonds
25g/1oz stem ginger – finely chopped
zest of 2 small lemons

juice of 1 lemon
1 dsp honey

Cream together the butter and sugar until light and fluffy.

In a separate bowl mix the coconut, almonds, baking powder, polenta and flour.

Add half of the eggs to the creamed butter and mix well, then add half of the flour mixture and mix again. Add the rest of the eggs and then the flour, mixing well after each addition. Now add the ginger and the zest of the lemons. Transfer to a lined round (18–20cm/7–8 inches) or rectangular (23 x 7.5/9 x 3 inches) baking tin and bake in the oven @ 180°C/gas mark 4 for 40–45 minutes until the cake is firm and cooked.

This cake can be decorated with toasted coconut or by heating the zest and juice of one lemon with 1 dsp honey. Allow the cake to cool slightly, then pierce the top several times with a skewer. Pour the honey and lemon syrup over the cake and let it absorb. If you can, prepare the cake two or three days in advance to allow the sponge to absorb the syrup completely.

gingered fruit
crème brûlée

570ml/1pt milk
1/2 vanilla pod – split
110g/4oz caster sugar
2 tbsp water
6 egg yolks
2 tbsp Marsala wine

110g/4oz assorted dried fruits,
   e.g. apricots, prunes, papaya,
   pears – finely chopped
2–4 dsp Marsala wine
25g/1oz stem ginger – finely
   chopped
50g/2oz granulated sugar

Serves 4

custard

Pour the milk into a saucepan and add the vanilla pod. Bring to the boil and then leave to one side to allow the vanilla flavour to infuse the milk.

Place half of the caster sugar and the water in a separate saucepan. Bring the mixture to the boil and continue boiling until the sugar and water turn a golden caramel colour. Remove the saucepan from the heat. After removing the vanilla pod from the milk, gently pour the sugar mixture into the milk. Now add the Marsala wine and stir.

Place the eggs yolks and the remaining caster sugar in a large bowl and whisk until the mixture becomes light and creamy. Now add this creamy mixture to the milk and leave to one side for 5 minutes to allow the flavours to infuse.

gingered fruit

Place the dried fruits, Marsala wine and ginger in a large bowl and mix well. Leave to one side for 10 minutes until the fruit has plumped up and absorbed all the flavours. Spoon the fruit into 4 individual ramekins, 7.5–10cm/3–4 inches in diameter, then pour in the custard until the ramekins are about two-thirds full. Place them in the oven at 150ºC/gas mark 2 for 45 minutes.

Remove from the oven and when cool, sprinkle with a layer of granulated sugar and place below a hot grill for a minute or so until golden and bubbling. The 'brûlée' effect may also be created by using the small blow torches that are now readily available in department stores and supermarkets.

If following a dairy-free diet, substitute soya milk or rice milk for the cow's milk.

This dessert is gently flavoured with the rich, smoky flavour of Marsala wine, a fortified wine produced in Marsala in Sicily. You only need to use a little of it in this recipe, but the wine keeps for a long time. It is well worth having Marsala wine in your cupboard as it can be used in all kinds of sauces and desserts.

apple, lemon and
vanilla cake

2–3 Bramley apples – sliced or diced
75g/3oz sultanas
75g/3oz muscatel raisins
2–3 dsp apple juice
zest of 1 lemon
few drops of vanilla essence

150ml /^{1}/4 pint olive or sunflower oil
50g /2oz soft brown sugar
50g /2oz caster sugar
2 eggs – lightly beaten
350g /12oz plain flour – sieved
1 ^{1}/2 tsp bicarbonate of soda
^{1}/2 tsp cream of tartar
1 tsp cinnamon
^{1}/2 tsp nutmeg
icing sugar for dusting

Lemon and vanilla work wonderfully well together in cake recipes. I've combined their flavours in this soft textured apple cake, which can be served either as a cake or as a pudding topped with cardamom-scented yoghurt. The butter in this recipe has been replaced with olive oil, so the fat content is relatively low.

In a large bowl place the dried fruits, apple juice, lemon zest and vanilla essence.

Mix well together and leave to infuse for approximately 15–20 minutes until the fruit has plumped up and softened. If you are pressed for time, warm the apple juice before adding to the fruit and the fruit should be plumped up in 5 minutes or so.

In a large bowl whisk together the oil and sugars for approximately 4–5 minutes until everything is well mixed. Add the eggs a little at a time and beat well after each addition. The mixture should now be light and frothy. Mix together the sieved flour, spices and raising agents and add to the bowl, in 3–4 stages, mixing gently after each addition until everything is well mixed. Now add the apples and the dried fruits and mix well. Transfer the cake mixture to a lined cake tin about 18–20cm/7–8 inches in diameter and bake in the oven @ 180°C/gas mark 4 for approximately 1 ^{1}/2 hours or until it is firm to the touch. Remove from the oven and dust with icing sugar.

Serve warm or cold. I prefer it warm and served with yoghurt.

With the wide variety of fruit now available, fruit salads are becoming increasingly popular. Not only are they easy to make and packed full of goodness, but they also look stunning.

warmed tropical
fruit
with caramel and coconut sauce

Serves 8

Prepare all the fruit before you begin to assemble this fruit salad.

Peel and slice the mango.

Peel the papaya, cut into half, remove the seeds, cut into slices and sprinkle with lime juice to develop the flavour.

Peel the banana, cut it into long slices and sprinkle with lemon juice to prevent browning.

Remove the stalk and hard skin from the pineapple. Cut into long strips, removing the woody core from the centre of the pineapple.

Scoop the melon into rounds or cut in chunks.

Peel the oranges and grapefruit, remove the pith carefully and divide into segments.

Cut the passion fruit in half. Scoop out and reserve the seeds and juice.

Arrange all the fruit in a large ovenproof dish. Mix the ginger, white rum and demerara sugar and sprinkle over the fruits. When ready to serve, place below a very hot grill for 2–3 minutes until the fruit is slightly blackened and sweetened.

1 ripe mango
2 small ripe papayas
juice of 1 lime
2 bananas
juice of 1 lemon
1/2 fresh pineapple (or 1 small one)
1 honeydew melon
2 oranges
1 pink grapefruit
2 passion fruit
1 inch root ginger – grated
2 dsp white rum
25g/1oz demerara sugar

caramel and coconut sauce

Heat the sugar and water together until the mixture is bubbling and golden. Add the coconut milk and stir and heat until the sauce is warmed through. Pour the warm sauce over the grilled fruit and serve immediately.

150g/5oz caster sugar
4 dsp water
125ml/4floz coconut milk

Yellowman is a traditional Irish sweet and is a speciality of Ballycastle in County Antrim. It is a type of chewy toffee with a distinctive yellow colour that gives it its name. In this recipe, just a little of this sweet is used as a topping to create a stunning dessert.

bittersweet tangy orange
mousse
with a crunchy topping of yellowman

Serves 8

the base

Place the nuts, biscuits, oil and marmalade in a saucepan and stir while cooking over a gentle heat. Cook for approximately 2 minutes until the mixture is slightly sticky, then place in a well-greased 18cm/7 inch round loose-bottomed flan dish. Pat down well and leave to cool.

50g/2oz pecans – finely chopped
110g/4oz low-fat digestive/ginger
  biscuits – crushed
1 dsp olive oil
1 tsp reduced-sugar marmalade

the mousse

Place the egg yolks and sugar in a bowl and cook for about 6–7 minutes over a saucepan of warm water, beating occasionally until the mixture becomes pale and slightly thick and loses its eggy flavour.

Beat the egg whites until stiff.

Sprinkle the gelatine over the orange juice in a bowl. Place the bowl in a saucepan of hot water for 2–3 minutes until the gelatine has dissolved completely. Remove the bowl from the saucepan.

Stir a spoonful of the cooked egg mixture into the gelatine. Add this to the rest of the egg mixture, then add the cream and yoghurt, orange zest and juice and mix well. Finally, gently fold in the egg whites. Pour the filling over the biscuit base and chill in the fridge for at least 3 hours.

4 eggs yolks
25g/1oz caster sugar
2 egg whites
25g/1oz powdered gelatine
juice of 1–2 oranges
55ml/2floz whipping cream and yoghurt
  – mixed
zest and juice of 2 oranges

to serve

When the mousse is cool and firm, decorate with crushed yellowman and orange zest or simply with orange zest. Garnish with mint and serve with yoghurt.

25g/1oz yellowman – crushed
zest of 1 orange – coarsely grated
sprigs of mint
Greek yoghurt

mixed berry crisp with
macadamia
nuts

This pudding looks stunning. It is served in individual bowls, packed with berries, and when cooked the juice oozes out over the crispy crumble. If possible, use berries that are ripe and in prime condition – the berries will then have just the right amount of sweetness and you will not need to use the additional sugar that I have included in the recipe.

110g/4oz flour
50g/2oz soft brown sugar
50g/2oz macadamia nuts
50g/2oz rolled oats
1/2 tsp cinnamon
50g/2oz butter – softened

25g/1oz arrowroot
125ml/1/4pt water
225g/8oz blackberries
110g/4oz currants
110g/4oz raspberries or blueberries
50g/2oz caster sugar
4 tbsp water
1/2 tsp cinnamon

mixed berry crisp

Place the flour, sugar, nuts, oats and cinnamon in a large bowl and mix well. Add the butter and mix well until it is completely incorporated. Set to one side.

the fruits

Mix together the arrowroot and water and set to one side for a moment. Place all the fruits in a large saucepan and add the sugar (if necessary), cinnamon and blended arrowroot. Bring the mixture to the boil and simmer gently for 1 minute.

Transfer the mixture to individual ramekins, approximately 7.5–10cm/3–4 inches in diameter. The ramekins should only be half-full. Spoon the crisp over the top and bake in the oven @ 190°C/gas mark 5 for 25 minutes.

Serve immediately with vanilla ice cream or frozen yoghurt.

Acknowledgements

As far as directors and publishers go, I have the best! Thank you all for letting me do what I believe in – this book has certainly been that.

I have managed to enlist the help and talents of many people. A big thank you to everyone for all your support and hard work. To Alan Bremner and Orla McKibbin at UTV; Bernie Morrison, producer and director of the television series; to the crew, Sam Christie, Ivan Heslip, Billy Rowan, Mary McCleave and tape editor Robert Hastings. Thanks also to the publishing team at Blackstaff Press, to photographer Robert McKeag and to food stylist Colette Coughlan. I am also grateful to Maureen Best, Nan Millar and Vera McCready for all their hard work behind the scenes and to Roisin O'Brien at Peter Mark, Ballymena.

Many thanks also to Helen Turkington at the Fabric Library, Cookstown and Newbridge, County Kildare; to Paddy McNeill of Beeswax, Kilrea, for sourcing the free-standing dressers and cupboards; to Sally at Floral Designs, Ballymena, for the flower arrangements; to Nicholas Mosse Pottery, Kilkenny; Christine Foy, Mullaghmeen Pottery, Enniskillen; Laura Ashley, Belfast; Le Creuset; Lakeland Limited; Hilary and Ian Robinson at Presence, Newtownards, for so much hard work in coordinating china, pottery and dishes for the programmes; to Freda Hayes and Paula O'Connell of Meadows and Byrne for props for food photography; to Sydney Stevenson Agencies, Bangor, and Meyer Prestige; to Weight Watchers, the Chest, Heart and Stroke Association, Diabetes UK and Coeliac UK for dietary advice; and to all the family and friends who contributed to the programme and helped to make it such an enjoyable experience.

Index